UNVEILING PRIVACY

SAFEGUARDING YOUR DIGITAL LIFE IN A DATA-DRIVEN WORLD

By:

Troy Williams

CONTENTS

INTRODUCTION: THE URGENCY OF PRIVACY IN THE DIGITAL AGE 5

    Set the Stage: The Critical Importance of Privacy Today 5

    Key Takeaways: 7

CHAPTER 1: UNDERSTANDING THE DIGITAL PRIVACY LANDSCAPE 9

    Overview 9

    The Three Major Threats to Digital Privacy 11

    Actionable Solutions to Protect Your Privacy 15

    Key Takeaways: 17

CHAPTER 2: THE ANATOMY OF A PRIVACY BREACH 20

    Overview: How Hackers and Corporations Exploit Personal Information 20

    Actionable Solutions: How to Spot and Avoid Phishing 23

    Actionable Solution: Use Antivirus Software 26

    Actionable Solution: Minimize Your Digital Footprint 32

    Key Takeaways: 33

CHAPTER 3: PROTECTING YOUR DIGITAL IDENTITY 35

    Overview: 35

    Why Multi-Factor Authentication (MFA) Is Essential 36

    Actionable Steps: 42

CHAPTER 4: CORPORATE SURVEILLANCE – HOW TO FIGHT BACK 44

Overview: How Corporations Track and Monetize Your Data 44

Actionable Solutions: Taking Back Control of Your Data 47

Key Takeaways: 50

CHAPTER 5: GOVERNMENT OVERREACH AND YOUR PRIVACY RIGHTS 52

Overview: The Delicate Balance Between National Security and Personal Privacy 52

What Is Government Overreach? 55

Recent Government Surveillance Cases and Their Global Impact.... 65

Key Takeaways: 68

CHAPTER 6: THE ROLE OF ARTIFICIAL INTELLIGENCE IN PRIVACY 71

Overview: AI-Driven Surveillance and Data Protection Tools 71

Actionable Solutions: Using AI-Powered Privacy Tools 76

Actionable Steps: 87

CHAPTER 7: BIOMETRIC DATA – THE NEW FRONTIER 89

Overview: The rise of biometric data in security and its privacy implications. 89

Actionable Solutions: Manage biometric data storage and usage and stay informed about biometric data laws. 95

Staying Informed About Biometric Data Laws 99

Key Takeaways: 103

CHAPTER 8: BUILDING A PRIVACY-FIRST LIFESTYLE 105

    Overview: Integrating Privacy into Your Daily Routine 105

    Actionable Solutions: Updating Privacy Settings, Educating Others, and Staying Informed on Privacy Tools 110

    Actionable Steps: 115

CHAPTER 9: FUTURE TRENDS IN PRIVACY – WHAT'S NEXT? 117

    Overview: Predict Future Developments in Privacy and Prepare for an Evolving Landscape 117

    Actionable Solutions: Staying Ahead of Trends and Embracing Privacy Innovations 122

CONCLUSION: RECLAIMING YOUR DIGITAL LIFE 130

    Key Takeaways: 136

U.S. PRIVACY LAWS AND ACTS 138

U.S. PRIVACY-RELATED ACRONYMS AND DEFINITIONS 142

APPENDICES 146

    Privacy Toolkit: A Curated List of Privacy-Enhancing Tools and Apps 146

    Glossary of Terms: Definitions of vital privacy-related terms 152

    Further Reading: Books, Articles, and Studies for Deeper Exploration of Digital Privacy 160

INTRODUCTION: THE URGENCY OF PRIVACY IN THE DIGITAL AGE

Set the Stage: The Critical Importance of Privacy Today

In an era dominated by digital transformation, privacy has evolved into something far more complex and critical than ever before. Once viewed as a personal right to keep certain aspects of one's life concealed from public view, privacy has become a fundamental issue in the digital age, with vast implications for our personal freedom, security, and even democracy. We live in a time where every action we take online—browsing a website, sending a message, or making a purchase—can be tracked, recorded, and analyzed. While these technological advancements offer convenience and connectivity, they expose us to unprecedented surveillance and data exploitation levels.

At the heart of this issue is the vast collection and monetization of personal data. Corporations, advertisers, and governments continuously gather our digital footprints, creating detailed profiles of our behaviors, preferences, and interactions. This data is then used to influence everything from the advertisements we see to the political content we're exposed to, potentially shaping our opinions and decisions without our conscious knowledge. The implications for individual autonomy and free will are profound, as our digital personas can be manipulated for commercial or political gain.

Moreover, the threat of data breaches and cyberattacks has never been more accurate. High-profile cases of hacked databases leaked personal information, and stolen identities are now commonplace, leading to financial losses, emotional distress, and long-term damage to individuals' reputations. For businesses, the stakes are equally high, as trust in digital systems and services is eroded with every new incident of compromised privacy. In the worst cases, this breach of confidence can lead to severe legal, financial, and reputational consequences for companies that fail to protect user data adequately.

Perhaps most concerning is the government's role in surveilling its citizens. Under the guise of national security, various governments worldwide have expanded their powers to monitor communications, collect personal data, and conduct mass surveillance on an unprecedented scale. While such measures are often justified by the need to combat terrorism and crime, they raise serious ethical questions about the balance between national security and the right to privacy. The potential for abuse is significant, as increased surveillance capabilities allow for greater control over the population, eroding civil liberties in the process.

In this digital age, privacy is no longer just about keeping our personal lives out of the public eye—it's about protecting the very foundations of our freedom, dignity, and democracy. As more of our lives move online, the importance of understanding, protecting, and reclaiming our privacy cannot be overstated. It's no longer a choice; it's a necessity.

This book addresses the importance of protecting our privacy in a digital world that thrives on data. As we navigate this new landscape, understanding how our data is collected, shared, and used is essential to safeguarding our identities and our freedom and autonomy. In a time when even our most intimate moments can be tracked, monitored, and stored, the need for privacy has never been more urgent.

Throughout this book, you will have the knowledge and tools to reclaim your privacy. Whether you're an everyday internet user, a privacy-conscious professional, or someone looking to understand how to protect your information, this book will guide you step-by-step through taking control of your digital life.

Key Takeaways:

- **Knowledge:** By the end of this book, you'll understand the vast landscape of digital privacy threats, from data breaches to corporate surveillance and government overreach.
- **Tools:** To help protect your information, you will be introduced to a wide array of privacy-enhancing tools, including secure browsers, encrypted messaging apps, and privacy-focused settings.
- **Confidence:** Privacy doesn't have to be a complicated, overwhelming task. You will gain the confidence to navigate the digital world with a clear understanding of safeguarding your data and empower yourself to make informed decisions about your privacy.

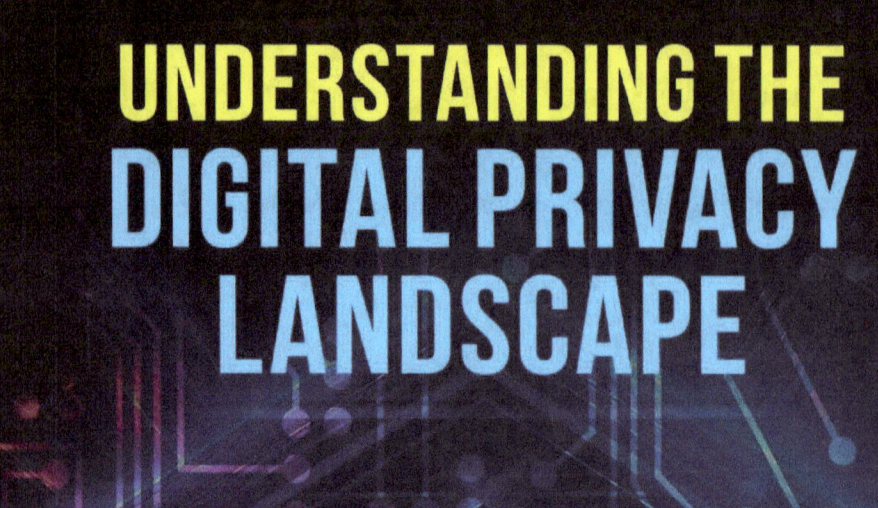

CHAPTER 1: UNDERSTANDING THE DIGITAL PRIVACY LANDSCAPE

Overview

In today's hyperconnected world, digital privacy has become a critical issue. As more people rely on the internet for nearly everything—communication, shopping, working, and even entertainment—the amount of personal data circulating online has reached unprecedented levels. This data includes sensitive information, such as our social security numbers, financial records, location data, and even private conversations. While technology offers convenience and access to global resources, it also creates significant risks. The more information we share online, the more vulnerable we become to privacy violations.

In this chapter, we will explore the three major threats to digital privacy: corporate surveillance, data breaches, and government overreach. But before we delve into these topics, it's essential to define what privacy means in the digital age and how the concept has evolved.

What Is Privacy?

In a traditional sense, privacy is often understood as the right to be left alone or to keep certain aspects of one's life away from public view. The dictionary defines privacy as "the state of being free from unwanted or unauthorized intrusion." For example, privacy allows you to sing in the shower or dance in your kitchen without the fear that someone is watching. It's about controlling what others can see, hear, or know about you.

However, in the digital age, privacy has become much more complicated. As more of our lives occur online, privacy doesn't just mean being free from physical intrusion. It now includes the right to control the collection and use of our personal information. But here's the tricky part: many of us are unaware of how much personal data we give away, and even when we are aware, we often have little control over it.

Privacy in the Digital Age

In the online world, privacy can feel like a distant memory. Everything we do online—from the websites we visit to the messages we send—creates a digital "footprint." This footprint includes information about our behaviors, preferences, locations, and identities. Think about the last time you searched for something on Google or liked a post on social media. Those actions are stored, and that data can be used to build a detailed profile about you.

Today's internet users have over 90 online accounts, which jumps to 130 accounts linked to a single email address in the US. This means we leave bits and pieces of our personal lives scattered across the internet daily. As more people work from home and use digital tools for personal and professional reasons, the line between personal and professional data is becoming increasingly blurred. This shift means that protecting digital privacy is not just about safeguarding personal information but also protecting our professional lives and identities.

The Three Major Threats to Digital Privacy

Now that we have a basic understanding of what privacy means in the digital age, let's explore the three major threats to our digital privacy: corporate surveillance, data breaches, and government overreach.

1. Corporate Surveillance

When we talk about corporate surveillance, we're referring to companies collecting massive amounts of personal data from their users. Many of the most popular online platforms—social media networks, search engines, and e-commerce websites—collect and analyze vast amounts of user data to improve their services, personalize user experiences, and, most importantly, sell targeted advertising.

The Business of Data is often called "the new oil" because of its immense value. Just like oil, data is a resource that drives modern economies. Companies collect data on their users' habits, preferences, and behaviors and use that data to make money. For example, whenever you search for something on Google or scroll through Facebook, those companies collect information about you. This might include your search terms, time on certain websites, location, and device type. Over time, these companies can build incredibly detailed profiles of who you are, what you like, and how you behave online.

But data collection doesn't stop there. Many companies sell this information to third parties, such as advertisers and data brokers, who use it to target you with personalized ads. This is why, after searching for a pair of shoes online, you might suddenly see ads for those shoes on every website you visit.

Unfortunately, most people know how much their personal information is collected and used. Even seemingly harmless data, like your shopping habits or browsing history, can be used to build a detailed profile that may influence everything from the ads you see to the prices you're offered for goods and services.

Loss of Autonomy One of the most significant ethical concerns with corporate surveillance is the loss of autonomy. When companies have access to so much personal data, they can influence our decisions—often without us even realizing it. For example, targeted ads can subtly push us to buy certain products or services or even adopt specific political views. Over time, this constant bombardment of tailored content can limit our ability to make independent choices.

In some cases, companies may even use data to manipulate user behavior, raising important questions about free will and how much we control our online experiences.

2. Data Breaches

While corporate surveillance poses a long-term privacy risk, data breaches often have immediate and devastating consequences. A data breach occurs when sensitive information is accessed by unauthorized individuals—usually for malicious purposes. This information can include names, addresses, social security numbers, credit card details, and other personal data that can be used for identity theft, financial fraud, or even blackmail.

The Growing Threat of Data Breaches In recent years, data breaches have become increasingly common, affecting some of the largest companies and institutions in the world. One of the most infamous breaches occurred in 2017 when Equifax, a central credit reporting agency, was hacked. This breach exposed the personal information of over 147 million Americans, including social security numbers, credit card details, and driver's license numbers.

The consequences for data breach victims can be severe. Many people don't realize that their personal information has been compromised until it's too late—for example, when they discover unauthorized charges on their bank accounts or find out that someone has applied for a loan in their name. Once personal data is stolen and sold on the dark web, it's nearly impossible to get it back, which makes prevention critical.

What Kind of Data Is Stolen?

Hackers are interested in a wide range of personal information. Some of the most common targets include:

- Financial Information: Credit card numbers, bank account details, and other financial records.
- Personal Information: Social security numbers, driver's license numbers, and addresses.
- Corporate Information: Customer records, intellectual property, and trade secrets.

Even seemingly insignificant data, such as email addresses or shopping histories, can be valuable to hackers. Email addresses can be used for phishing scams, while purchase histories can be used to create fake accounts.

Causes of Data Breaches

Causes of Data Breaches Data breaches can occur for many reasons. In some cases, they result from sophisticated cyberattacks that exploit vulnerabilities in a company's security systems. For example, hackers may use malware to infiltrate a network or send phishing emails to trick employees into revealing sensitive information. In other cases, data breaches are caused by human error—such as accidentally sending sensitive information to the wrong person or failing to update security protocols.

Regardless of how they occur, data breaches are often catastrophic for individuals whose data is stolen and the companies that suffer the breach. Companies may face financial losses, reputational damage, and legal consequences, while individuals may experience identity theft, financial fraud, and emotional distress.

3. Government Overreach

In addition to corporate surveillance and data breaches, government surveillance is another major threat to privacy. Governments worldwide monitor their citizens for various reasons, including national security, law enforcement, and counterterrorism. While some level of government surveillance may be necessary to protect public safety, there is a growing concern that many governments are overstepping their bounds and infringing on individual rights.

Mass Surveillance Programs One of the most notorious examples of government overreach is the US National Security Agency's (NSA) PRISM program, which was revealed by whistleblower Edward Snowden in 2013. This program allowed the NSA to collect vast amounts of data from major tech companies, including emails, search histories, and phone records. Importantly, this data was collected without the explicit consent of the individuals involved, raising serious questions about the balance between privacy and security.

Similar mass surveillance programs exist in other countries as well. Governments often justify these programs by claiming they are necessary to prevent terrorism, enforce laws, and protect national security. However, critics argue that such programs can be easily abused, leading to widespread invasions of privacy.

Outdated Privacy Laws One of the challenges in addressing government surveillance is that many privacy laws are obsolete and haven't kept pace with technological advancements. For example, laws written before the digital age may not adequately address how modern technology allows for collecting, storing, and analyzing personal data. As a result, individuals may be left vulnerable to privacy violations by both governments and corporations.

In recent years, there have been efforts to update privacy laws to reflect the realities of the digital age. One example is the General Data Protection Regulation (GDPR) in the European Union, which aims to give individuals more control over their data. However, enforcement of these laws can be inconsistent, and many governments continue to engage in questionable surveillance practices.

Actionable Solutions to Protect Your Privacy

Despite the challenges posed by corporate surveillance, data breaches, and government overreach, there are steps you can take to protect your privacy in the digital age. Here are some practical solutions:

1. **Conduct a Personal Data Audit**

Start by understanding what information about you is already available online. Conducting a personal data audit will help you take stock of your digital footprint and identify areas where you can improve your privacy.

- **Review Your Social Media Profiles:** Check the privacy settings on your social media accounts and remove any unnecessary personal information, such as your location, contact details, or employment history.
- **Search for Your Name Online:** Perform a web search for your name to see what information is publicly available. If you find sensitive data, contact the websites to request its removal.
- **Review Data-Sharing Agreements:** Review the privacy policies and terms of service for websites and apps you use to understand how your data is collected and shared.

2. **Use Privacy Tools**

Several tools can help enhance your privacy online by blocking trackers, encrypting communications, and securing your online activities.

- **Use a VPN:** A Virtual Private Network (VPN) encrypts your internet connection and hides your IP address, making it more difficult for third parties to track your online activities.
- **Install a Secure Browser:** Privacy-focused browsers like Brave and Firefox and privacy extensions like uBlock Origin and Privacy Badger can block tracking cookies and prevent advertisers from following your online movements.

- **Use Encrypted Messaging Apps:** Apps like Signal and Telegram offer end-to-end encryption, ensuring your conversations remain private and secure.

3. Set Up Privacy-Focused Social Media Settings

Social media platforms are some of the biggest culprits in data collection. However, by adjusting your privacy settings, you can limit the amount of personal information shared with third parties.

- **Restrict Who Can See Your Posts:** On platforms like Facebook, Instagram, and Twitter, you can adjust your account settings to control who can view your posts, photos, and personal information.
- **Limit App Permissions:** Review the permissions granted to apps connected to your social media accounts and revoke access for any apps that do not need your data.
- **Opt-Out of Data-Sharing Programs:** Many social media platforms participate in data-sharing agreements with third-party advertisers. Opting out of these programs can help prevent your information from being used for targeted ads.

Key Takeaways:

- **Audit your online presence**: Regularly check what personal information is publicly available about you and adjust privacy settings accordingly.
- **Limit data sharing**: Be mindful of the personal data you share on social media, apps, and websites.

- **Use privacy-focused tools**: Switch to browsers and search engines that prioritize privacy, such as Brave or DuckDuckGo.

- **Opt-out of data collection**: Take advantage of opt-out services that allow you to remove your data from corporate tracking databases.

- **Enable two-factor authentication (2FA)**: Add an extra layer of security to all your accounts.

THE ANATOMY OF A PRIVACY BREACH

CHAPTER 2: THE ANATOMY OF A PRIVACY BREACH

Overview: How Hackers and Corporations Exploit Personal Information

In today's digital world, privacy breaches are a severe threat, with hackers and corporations using various methods to gather and manipulate personal information. While hackers often aim to steal sensitive data, corporations may use it to track consumer behavior for profit. Understanding how these breaches happen is crucial to protecting your digital privacy.

Hackers typically exploit individuals through phishing, malware, and data mining. Meanwhile, corporations employ invasive data collection and sharing practices. This chapter will explore these methods in detail, discuss real-world examples, and offer actionable tips to help safeguard personal data.

Phishing Attacks: A Common Gateway to Breaches

Phishing is one of the most common methods cybercriminals use to steal personal information. It tricks people into believing they interact with a legitimate source—like their bank, a trusted retailer, or a social media platform. This deception often leads to revealing sensitive details, such as login credentials, Social Security numbers, or credit card information. Phishing attacks usually arrive in emails, text messages, or fake websites that closely resemble the real thing.

The main goal of phishing is simple:

- Steal personal data.
- Gain access to your accounts.
- Use that data for financial gain or identity theft.

Once hackers access sensitive information, they can sell it on the dark web, commit fraud, or even infect your device with malware.

How Phishing Works:

Phishing plays a role in human trust. We instinctively trust familiar institutions like banks and online platforms, which phishers exploit by mimicking these sources.

- **The Email Trap:** One common phishing tactic is sending an email that looks like it's from a reputable organization, such as your bank. The email might say, "We've detected suspicious activity on your account. Please verify your identity by clicking the link below." This message often creates a sense of urgency, pressuring you to act quickly without considering if the email is genuine. Once you click the link, you're taken to a fake website that looks almost identical to the real one. When you enter your information, you unknowingly hand it to hackers.
- **Spear-Phishing:** Personalized Attacks: Unlike standard phishing, spear-phishing is more targeted. Attackers research their victims and tailor their messages to look even more legitimate. For example, they may use your name, job title, or specific details about your life. An email might come from what looks like your company's HR department, mentioning a recent policy update.

Since the message feels personal, you're more likely to trust and act on it.

- **Whaling:** Targeting High-Profile Individuals: Whaling is a specialized spear-phishing aimed at high-profile targets, such as executives or politicians. These attacks often involve more sophisticated methods, as the stakes are higher. For example, a CEO may receive an email that appears to come from another executive or a business partner requesting sensitive financial information. The consequences of a successful whaling attack can be devastating, both for the individual and their organization.

Why Phishing Works:

Phishing works by tapping into critical psychological triggers, such as fear and urgency. Here are some common tactics phishers use:

- **Fear of Losing Access:** Phishers often create urgency by warning that your account will be locked or compromised unless you act quickly. This fear causes victims to respond without verifying if the message is legitimate.
- **Incentives and Rewards:** Some phishing messages promise rewards, like lottery winnings or exclusive offers. These offers match your desire for easy money, making you more likely to click.
- **Authority Figures:** Emails that appear to come from trusted institutions, like your bank or employer, are often harder to question. Phishers use this trust to make their messages seem more convincing.

Real-Life Phishing Examples:

Phishing attacks have had severe consequences in real life. Let's look at two significant examples:

1. **The 2016 DNC Email Hack:** During the 2016 US presidential election, hackers targeted the Democratic National Committee (DNC) using spear-phishing tactics. John Podesta, chairman of Hillary Clinton's campaign, received an email that looked like a security alert from Google. He clicked the link and reset his password, unknowingly giving hackers access to his account. This breach led to the leaking of sensitive emails, which had political repercussions.
2. **COVID-19 Pandemic Scams:** During the pandemic, phishing attacks skyrocketed. Cybercriminals sent fake emails claiming to offer COVID-19 relief funds or vaccine appointments, tricking people into giving away their personal information. These emails often mimicked government agencies or health organizations, making them appear credible.

Actionable Solutions: How to Spot and Avoid Phishing

Phishing attacks are avoidable if you know the warning signs. Here's how you can protect yourself:

1. **Verify the Sender:** Always double-check the sender's email address before clicking on any links. Phishers often use addresses similar to real ones but with slight differences (e.g., support@yourbank-secure.com instead of support@yourbank.com).

2. **Look for Red Flags:** Look for poor grammar, generic greetings like "Dear customer," and a sense of urgency. Legitimate companies usually address you by name and maintain a professional tone.
3. **Hover Over Links:** Hover over links to see the URL before clicking any link. Don't click if it doesn't match the official website or looks suspicious.
4. **Avoid Downloading Attachments:** Be wary of downloading attachments from unknown sources. Phishing emails often include attachments that can install malware on your device.
5. Enable Two-Factor Authentication (2FA): Using 2FA adds an extra layer of security to your accounts. Even if a phisher gets your password, they won't be able to access your account without a second form of authentication.
6. **Report Phishing Attempts:** Report suspicious emails to your email provider or the company being impersonated. Many organizations have dedicated phishing hotlines to help stop these attacks.

Malware: The Hidden Threat

Malware is software designed to infiltrate and damage systems without your consent. While viruses are the most well-known type of malware, others—like worms, Trojans, ransomware, spyware, and adware—are just as dangerous.

These malicious programs can steal sensitive information, damage systems, or extort money. The damage caused by malware can be extensive, ranging from identity theft to major operational disruptions.

Types of Malware:

- **Viruses:** Viruses attach themselves to legitimate files or programs and spread when those files are opened. They can slow down your computer, delete important files, or crash entire systems. Viruses often require user interaction to spread.
- **Worms:** Unlike viruses, worms can replicate and spread across networks without user interaction. They exploit security flaws in software and can cause significant damage by slowing down networks or crashing servers.
- **Trojans:** Trojans disguise themselves as legitimate software, tricking users into downloading them. Once installed, they can steal sensitive data, open backdoors for other malware, or give attackers remote access to the system.
- **Ransomware:** Ransomware locks or encrypts files, making them inaccessible until a ransom is paid, often in cryptocurrency. Even paying the ransom doesn't guarantee that your files will be recovered. Ransomware attacks have hit hospitals, businesses, and individuals, usually causing significant financial and operational damage.
- **Spyware:** Spyware monitors your activities without your knowledge, collecting sensitive information like passwords, credit card details, and browsing history. This information can be used for identity theft or sold to third parties.
- **Adware:** While not as harmful as other types of malware, adware can compromise your privacy by tracking your browsing habits and showing unwanted ads. It can also slow down your device and expose you to more severe threats.

The Real-world Impact of Malware

Malware infections can have long-term consequences for individuals and businesses alike. For individuals, the damage might include identity theft, financial fraud, or exposure of sensitive personal information. On the other hand, companies may face data breaches, loss of intellectual property, and damage to their reputation. In either case, the recovery cost can be high financially and in terms of trust.

For example, the 2017 WannaCry ransomware attack affected over 230,000 computers worldwide, including critical systems within the UK's National Health Service (NHS). Hospitals were forced to cancel surgeries, and emergency patients had to be diverted as systems were rendered inoperable. This attack highlighted the severe risks posed by cyberattacks, not just to data but also to human lives.

Actionable Solution: Use Antivirus Software

Reliable antivirus software is one of the most basic yet essential tools for defending against malware. Originally designed to detect, block, and remove malicious software from your system, antivirus programs have evolved into powerful shields that protect users from various online threats.

Modern antivirus software scans files and compares them to a database of known malware signatures. However, it doesn't stop there—most advanced antivirus programs now incorporate heuristic analysis, meaning they can identify potentially harmful behaviors, even if the malware has not been previously recognized or officially cataloged. By detecting suspicious patterns, they catch new or disguised malware that might otherwise slip through the cracks.

Several highly reputable antivirus programs are available, each offering unique features and varying levels of protection. Among the best are Bitdefender, Norton, Kaspersky, and Malwarebytes. When selecting antivirus software, it is essential to look for features such as real-time protection, automatic updates, and the ability to quarantine and remove malware. These features help ensure that your system remains secure even as new threats emerge.

1. Regular Scans and Updates

Installing antivirus software isn't enough—you must also schedule regular system scans. These scans can catch malware that bypassed real-time defenses or infected your system before the antivirus software was updated. Running periodic complete system scans ensures that hidden threats are uncovered and removed.

Equally important is keeping your antivirus software updated. Cybercriminals are constantly developing new forms of malware, and antivirus providers release updates to keep up with these evolving threats. An outdated antivirus program might fail to detect newer malware strains, leaving your system vulnerable to infection.

In addition to antivirus software, regularly updating your operating system and software applications is critical. Malware often exploits known vulnerabilities in outdated software. Software developers frequently release patches to address these vulnerabilities, but users who delay or skip updates risk falling victim to preventable attacks.

Take the WannaCry attack as an example. This ransomware targeted computers running outdated versions of Windows. Although Microsoft had released a security patch months before the attack, many systems remained unpatched and vulnerable. Those who had updated their software were immune to the ransomware, demonstrating how crucial it is to stay current with software updates.

To avoid such risks, enable automatic updates wherever possible. If automatic updates are not feasible, make it a habit to manually check for updates regularly.

Additional Precautions Against Malware

While antivirus software and updates provide significant protection, you can take other essential steps to minimize your malware infection risk further.

- **Avoid Untrusted Downloads and Links:** Malware often disguises itself as legitimate files, such as email attachments or software downloads. To avoid this, be cautious when downloading files or clicking links from unknown sources. Stick to official websites or trusted platforms when downloading software, and verify the legitimacy of emails, especially those containing attachments or links.
- **Use Strong Passwords and Multi-Factor Authentication (MFA):** Many malware infections, especially ransomware and Trojans, rely on gaining access to user accounts. Weak passwords make it easy for attackers to breach these accounts. Use strong, unique passwords for every account, and consider using a password manager to help keep track of them. Enable MFA wherever possible to provide extra protection, even if your password is compromised.

- **Backup Your Data Regularly:** If malware does manage to infiltrate your system, having recent backups of your important files can be a lifesaver. Ransomware, in particular, can be mitigated if you have secure, up-to-date backups stored on an external device or a cloud service that isn't directly connected to your primary system. Regular backups ensure that, in the worst-case scenario, you can recover your data without paying a ransom or facing significant data loss.

Data Mining: Corporate Surveillance at Its Worst

While malware attacks are direct and malicious, corporate data mining represents a more insidious invasion of privacy. Rather than stealing data outright, corporations subtly exploit personal information by collecting, analyzing, and monetizing it. This practice, known as data mining, involves collecting massive amounts of data about individuals to uncover patterns and behaviors to predict future actions, target advertisements, and influence decisions.

The Invasion of Your Private World

Every time you browse the internet, purchase, or interact on social media, you generate data. Corporations eagerly collect this data to build detailed profiles about you—profiles that reveal more than you may realize. Companies track nearly every aspect of your behavior, from favorite foods to political leanings.

Consider social media platforms like Facebook and Instagram. Every post you like, share, or comment on contributes to a detailed profile of your preferences, habits, and interests. These platforms track your interactions to serve you personalized ads. Have you ever noticed a product ad right after searching for it online? That's data mining at work.

The Dangers of Data Sharing and Breaches

The problem isn't just that companies collect this data—they share or sell it to third parties, often without your knowledge or consent. Many companies share your data with advertisers, analytics firms, and governments. While companies claim that the data they sell is anonymized, there have been numerous cases where it was re-identified, exposing the individuals behind the information.

Moreover, if a company storing your data is hacked, your personal information could be exposed in a data breach. Major corporations such as Facebook, Google, and Marriott have suffered breaches that compromised the sensitive data of millions of users. This data often ends up on the dark web, used for identity theft, fraud, or other forms of cybercrime.

For example, in 2018, Facebook was embroiled in the Cambridge Analytica scandal, in which the political consulting firm harvested data from over 87 million users without their consent. This data was then used to influence voter behavior in the 2016 US presidential election and the Brexit referendum. This incident illustrates how data mining invades individual privacy and can potentially manipulate entire societies.

The Impact of Predictive Analytics

Predictive analytics, a powerful tool in data mining, allows companies to forecast your future behavior based on your past actions. This can be convenient, such as when an online retailer suggests products based on your purchase history, but it also raises concerns about autonomy and manipulation.

For instance, insurance companies use predictive analytics to determine how likely you are to file a claim. If the data suggests a high risk, they may raise your premiums or deny coverage. Similarly, employers use predictive algorithms to screen job applicants, sometimes rejecting candidates based on arbitrary factors like the time of day they applied.

As predictive analytics evolves, the line between personalization and manipulation becomes increasingly blurred. The more companies know about you, the more they can influence your decisions—often without you even realizing it.

The Legal and Ethical Concerns

The widespread practice of data mining raises significant legal and ethical questions. Do users fully understand their consent when signing up for online services? Privacy policies are often long, complicated, and filled with legal jargon that few people take the time to read. Even when opt-out mechanisms exist, they are usually buried deep in settings and hard to find.

Moreover, there is little transparency about how companies collect, store, and share data. This lack of transparency undermines trust and makes it difficult for users to control their personal information.

Several governments have implemented privacy laws designed to protect consumers in response to these concerns. The General Data Protection Regulation (GDPR) in the European Union and the California Consumer Privacy Act (CCPA) are examples of such legislation. These laws require companies to be more transparent about their data practices and give consumers greater control over their data, including the right to access, correct, or delete it.

However, the internet's global nature complicates these protections. Data collected in one country can be transferred and used in another, often with weaker privacy protections. This creates loopholes that companies can exploit, leaving consumers with limited options for recourse when their data is mishandled.

Actionable Solution: Minimize Your Digital Footprint

To protect your privacy and reduce your exposure to data mining, you must minimize the personal information you share online. Here are several practical steps you can take:

- **Review Privacy Settings:** Regularly review the privacy settings on your social media accounts and online services. Limit who can see your posts and avoid sharing unnecessary personal details, such as your location, relationship status, or birthday.
- **Use Privacy-Focused Browsers:** Consider using browsers like Brave or Mozilla Firefox with privacy-enhancing extensions such as uBlock Origin, Privacy Badger, or Ghostery. These tools block trackers, ads, and third-party cookies, reducing the amount of data collected about you.
- **Opt-Out of Data Sharing:** Many companies offer the option to opt out of data sharing programs, although this option is often hidden in the fine print. Take the time to find these settings and opt out wherever possible. Services like Google and Facebook

also offer privacy dashboards where you can manage your data preferences.

- **Use a VPN:** A Virtual Private Network (VPN) encrypts your internet traffic and masks your IP address, making it more difficult for websites and third parties to track your online activities. VPNs are beneficial when using public Wi-Fi networks, as they add a layer of security and privacy.

- **Limit Permissions for Third-Party Apps:** Be cautious when granting apps access to your contacts, location, or other sensitive information. Restrict permissions to only what is necessary for the app to function, and regularly review the apps you've installed to ensure they're not overstepping.

Key Takeaways:

- **Recognize phishing attacks**: Be cautious of unsolicited emails, texts, or calls requesting personal information.

- **Use solid and unique passwords**: Ensure each account has a distinct password, and use a password manager to store them securely.

- **Regularly update software**: Keep your operating system and applications updated to patch security vulnerabilities.

- **Limit sharing sensitive information**: Avoid providing unnecessary details online, especially on unsecured websites.

- **Enable data breach alerts**: Sign up for alerts that notify you if your data is compromised in a breach.

PROTECTING YOUR DIGITAL IDENTITY

CHAPTER 3: PROTECTING YOUR DIGITAL IDENTITY

Overview:

In today's interconnected digital world, protecting one's identity has evolved from a personal responsibility to an essential survival skill. The rising reliance on online platforms for banking, shopping, social interaction, and even remote work has made our data—such as Social Security numbers, banking details, and other sensitive information—a prime target for cybercriminals. Identity theft is not just a distant threat; it is a growing reality with potentially devastating consequences, ranging from financial loss to irreversible damage to one's reputation.

Fortunately, safeguarding your digital identity is well within your control. With the proper knowledge and applying a few essential security practices, you can drastically minimize the risk of compromised identity. This chapter outlines practical steps to protect sensitive information and secure digital footprints.

The Growing Threat of Identity Theft

As technology advances, so do the methods employed by cybercriminals. Gone are the days when identity theft primarily involved stolen wallets and physical documents. Today, cybercriminals employ sophisticated techniques such as phishing attacks, data breaches, malware, and ransomware to access personal data. Protecting critical information—

such as your Social Security number, banking details, and passwords—has become more crucial than ever.

Your Social Security number (SSN) is one of your most valuable information. Often referred to as the "keys to the kingdom," your SSN provides access to a wide range of your personal and financial data, including your credit report, tax information, and medical records. Once cybercriminals gain access to this information, they can wreak havoc by opening credit accounts in your name, filing fraudulent tax returns, and more. Therefore, safeguarding your Social Security number should be a top priority in protecting your digital identity.

Your banking details are equally vulnerable. With the shift toward online and mobile banking, sensitive financial information is transmitted across networks, sometimes with security vulnerabilities. Losing control of your banking credentials can result in unauthorized withdrawals, fraudulent purchases, and long-term credit damage. Thus, protecting your banking details is critical to maintaining financial security in the digital age.

Why Multi-Factor Authentication (MFA) Is Essential

Enabling multi-factor authentication (MFA) on your accounts is a highly effective yet simple way to protect your digital identity. MFA requires two or more verification forms before allowing access to an account. Typically, it involves something you know (like a password), something you have (like a smartphone), and sometimes something you are (like biometric data).

MFA adds a vital extra layer of protection. Even if someone manages to steal your password, they still need a secondary form of authentication—such as a one-time passcode sent to your phone or a biometric scan—to access your account. This makes it nearly impossible for cybercriminals to access your sensitive information, even if they have your login credentials.

Many platforms, from social media sites to email providers and banking apps, offer MFA as an option, yet not everyone takes advantage of it. Setting up MFA is straightforward and often takes only a few minutes.

Here are some common forms of multi-factor authentication:

1. **SMS-based verification:** A one-time code is sent to your mobile device, which you must enter along with your password.
2. **App-based verification:** Apps like Google Authenticator generate a random code every few seconds, which you must input in addition to your password.
3. **Biometric authentication:** Some services allow you to use your fingerprint, facial recognition, or voice patterns as an additional authentication method.

Enabling MFA on all your essential accounts significantly reduces the risk of unauthorized access. Even if a hacker gets your password, the additional authentication step is a substantial barrier, ensuring your account stays secure.

Setting Up Banking Alerts: Staying One Step Ahead

Another crucial aspect of protecting your digital identity is staying informed about any unusual activity in your financial accounts. In today's fast-paced digital economy, monitoring your bank account in real-time can be challenging. This is where banking alerts can be a lifesaver.

Most banks now offer customizable alerts via email or text messages that notify you immediately when suspicious activity is on your account. These alerts can range from informing you about large withdrawals to alerting you of logins from unfamiliar devices or changes to your account settings. Setting up these alerts helps you stay one step ahead of potential threats.

Here's why setting up banking alerts is essential:

1. **Immediate notification:** In case of unauthorized activity, real-time alerts enable you to take immediate action, limiting the extent of the damage.
2. **Account security:** Banking alerts can inform you of password changes, new linked devices, or any unauthorized changes to your account settings, allowing you to safeguard your banking details.
3. **Fraud prevention:** Real-time updates help you catch potentially fraudulent activity early and report it to your bank, minimizing damage.

Setting up these alerts is simple. Most banks offer customizable options that allow you to decide which activities you want to be notified about. It's a good idea to enable alerts for large transactions, account setting changes, and new logins from unfamiliar devices. These alerts are an extra layer of protection, keeping you informed about what's happening with your accounts.

The Power of Strong and Unique Passwords

In the digital world, passwords are often the first defense against cyber threats. Yet, many people still use weak passwords or, even worse, the same password across multiple platforms. This makes it easier for cybercriminals to exploit these vulnerabilities and access sensitive information.

There are several common mistakes when it comes to password security:

- **Using weak or easily guessable passwords:** Passwords like "123456" or "password" are still alarmingly common and can be cracked in seconds. It's important to avoid using personal information such as your name or birthdate in your passwords.
- **Reusing passwords across multiple accounts:** If a cybercriminal manages to hack one account, they can use the same password to gain access to your other accounts.
- **Storing passwords insecurely:** Writing down passwords or saving them in an unsecured document makes them vulnerable to theft.

To create a solid and secure password:

- **Use a mix of characters:** Combine uppercase and lowercase letters, numbers, and special characters to make your password harder to crack.
- **Make it long:** The longer the password, the more secure it is. Aim for at least 12 characters.
- **Avoid common words and sequences:** Avoid dictionary words, names, or patterns like "qwerty" or "1111."
- **Consider using a passphrase:** A passphrase combines unrelated words and symbols, such as *"GreenTiger$56&Rain."*

Equally important is the practice of regularly updating your passwords. If you suspect that your information has been compromised or a company you use experiences a data breach, changing your passwords is essential as soon as possible. Regularly updating your passwords limits the chances of someone gaining long-term access to your accounts.

Using a Password Manager for Efficiency and Security

Given the sheer number of online accounts most people manage today, keeping track of multiple strong passwords can be daunting. A password manager can simplify your life while also enhancing your digital security. It securely stores all your passwords in an encrypted vault, allowing you to retrieve them quickly when needed.

Here are some key benefits of using a password manager:

- **Secure storage:** Password managers store your login credentials using encryption, meaning only you can access them.
- **Auto-fill feature:** Many password managers automatically fill in your login credentials when you visit a website, reducing the risk of typos or incorrect entries.
- **Generates strong passwords:** Password managers can generate strong, unique passwords for each account, ensuring that none of your accounts share the same password.

Popular password managers like LastPass, 1Password, and Bitwarden offer both free and premium versions, making them accessible to individual users and businesses alike. Using a password manager removes the need to rely on weak, easy-to-guess passwords or to remember multiple complex passwords across different platforms.

Securing Your Social Security Number: Best Practices

Your Social Security number is among the most valuable personal information a cybercriminal could obtain. If your SSN falls into the wrong hands, it can lead to a host of problems, including identity theft and fraud. Therefore, protecting your SSN is critical to maintaining your digital identity.

Here are some best practices to follow:

- **Limit sharing your SSN:** Only provide your Social Security number when necessary. Some organizations may request it, but it's important to ask why they need it and whether alternative identification forms are acceptable.
- **Shred documents containing your SSN:** Physical documents that include your SSN, such as tax documents and medical records, should be shredded before disposal to prevent identity theft.
- **Monitor your credit report regularly:** Continuously checking your credit report ensures that no unauthorized accounts have been opened in your name. Early detection of fraudulent activity can prevent long-term damage.
- **Sign up for identity theft protection services:** Services like LifeLock and IdentityForce can help monitor your Social Security number and notify you if any suspicious activity occurs. These services provide an extra layer of protection by continuously scanning various databases for potential misuse of your identity.

These best practices can safeguard your Social Security number and reduce identity theft risk.

Actionable Steps:

- **Use multi-factor authentication (MFA)**: Enable MFA on all your essential accounts for added protection.

- **Monitor your financial accounts**: Set up alerts for unusual activity on your bank and credit card accounts.

- **Regularly review credit reports**: Check your credit reports for any signs of identity theft or fraud.

- **Secure your Social Security Number (SSN)**: Only share your SSN when necessary, and monitor its use.

- **Use a password manager**: Store all your passwords securely and generate strong passwords for new accounts.

CORPORATE SURVEILLANCE
HOW TO FIGHT BACK

CHAPTER 4: CORPORATE SURVEILLANCE – HOW TO FIGHT BACK

Overview: How Corporations Track and Monetize Your Data

Corporations have perfected sophisticated strategies for tracking and monetizing individuals' data in today's digital world. Every click, scroll, and search leaves behind a digital footprint that companies capture, analyze, and transform into profit. The driving force behind this corporate surveillance is straightforward data, which means money. Companies can precisely target advertisements, personalize services, and increase revenue by collecting vast information about user behaviors, preferences, and activities.

This chapter delves into how corporations track data through cookies, pixel tags, and device fingerprinting. It also explores the implications of corporate surveillance, highlighting the risks it poses to your privacy and, more importantly, provides actionable solutions to help you regain control over your personal information. Data monetization goes beyond simple advertising—it can influence everything from how products are designed to how services are priced. It even plays a role in shaping political discourse and social movements. As privacy concerns grow and public awareness rises, understanding how companies surveil individuals and how to counteract this surveillance is essential.

The Rise of Corporate Surveillance

Corporate surveillance isn't a recent phenomenon—it has evolved as companies have discovered the immense value of user data. In the early stages of the Internet, businesses relied on simple analytics to track basic website performance metrics. Over time, however, these tracking systems became much more complex and capable of monitoring nearly every digital interaction. Today, tech giants like Google, Facebook, and Amazon have built their empires on the data they gather from users, generating billions of dollars in revenue.

Data points are collected whenever you interact with a digital platform—whether visiting a website, shopping online, or using an app. These data points may include your location, browsing habits, preferences, and spending patterns. Companies either sell this data to advertisers or use it to create highly tailored ads and content. The ultimate objective is to build detailed profiles of users, allowing companies to predict future behavior and influence decisions. Corporate surveillance doesn't just stop at knowing what you did online yesterday—it aims to predict what you'll do tomorrow.

One of the most common methods corporations use to track users is cookies. Cookies are small bits of data stored on your device when you visit a website. They help websites remember preferences, enhancing the user experience. However, they also allow companies to follow your activities across multiple sites, creating a detailed picture of your online behavior—a practice known as third-party tracking.

Another popular tracking tool is the pixel tag, a web beacon. These tiny, often invisible images are embedded in websites and emails to track user behavior. Whenever you visit a webpage or open an email, the pixel tag sends information back to the company, such as your IP address, device type, and browsing patterns. This data is often used to personalize marketing campaigns and segment user groups for targeted advertising.

Lastly, device fingerprinting is another insidious form of tracking. This method involves gathering unique details about your device, such as its operating system, browser type, and screen resolution. By piecing together these seemingly harmless details, companies can create a "fingerprint" for your device, allowing them to continue tracking you even if you clear cookies or use private browsing modes.

Why Corporate Surveillance is Concerning

The most troubling aspect of corporate surveillance is that it frequently occurs without explicit user consent. Although companies often require you to agree to privacy policies and terms of service, these documents are usually long, jargon-filled, and challenging to understand. Most users click "accept" without fully grasping what they consent to, allowing corporations to collect and use their data with little resistance.

Moreover, the data collected isn't solely used for targeted advertising. It influences everything from pricing services to how online content is customized for each user. In some instances, data collected through corporate surveillance has been weaponized to manipulate political opinions and influence elections. The infamous Cambridge Analytica scandal, where data harvested from Facebook was used to sway voters in political campaigns, is a stark example of how corporate data can be misused.

Another significant concern is the potential for data breaches. The more data companies collect, the greater the risk of compromised information. High-profile breaches, such as those involving Equifax and Facebook, have exposed the personal information of millions of people, leading to identity theft, financial fraud, and long-term harm for the individuals affected.

Actionable Solutions: Taking Back Control of Your Data

Even though corporate surveillance is pervasive, there are practical steps you can take to reduce your digital footprint and regain control over your personal information. By using privacy-enhancing tools, adjusting settings on your devices, and being mindful of the data you share, you can significantly limit how much information companies collect about you.

1. **Using Browser Extensions to Block Tracking**

One of the most straightforward ways to limit corporate tracking is to install browser extensions to block trackers and advertisements. These extensions can prevent cookies, pixel tags, and other tracking methods from functioning, significantly reducing the data collected about your online behavior.

- **uBlock Origin:** An open-source extension that efficiently blocks ads and trackers without slowing your browsing experience. It is customizable, allowing users to create filters tailored to their needs, making it a powerful tool in the fight against surveillance.
- **Privacy Badger:** Developed by the Electronic Frontier Foundation (EFF), Privacy Badger automatically learns to block

invisible trackers as you browse. It becomes more effective over time, continuously improving its ability to protect your privacy.

- **Ghostery:** This extension blocks tracking scripts and offers insights into which trackers are trying to monitor your activity. It also has a feature that anonymizes your data, making it harder for corporations to collect personal information.
- **HTTPS Everywhere:** This tool ensures your connection to websites is secure by forcing the use of HTTPS, which encrypts your data. This prevents third parties from intercepting your information, providing additional security while browsing.

These tools can drastically reduce the amount of data companies collect about you. However, some websites may block access if they detect an ad blocker, so you might need to turn off your blocker temporarily to view certain content.

2. Opting Out of Data Collection Programs

Many companies allow users to opt out of data collection, but these options are often hidden deep within privacy settings. By actively seeking out these settings and adjusting them, you can significantly reduce the amount of personal information gathered.

- **Google Privacy Settings:** As one of the most prominent data collectors, Google allows you to limit its data collection through privacy settings. You can turn off personalized ads, stop location tracking, and pause monitoring of your web and app activity. Additionally, Google allows you to review and delete previously stored data, such as your search history and location records.

- **Facebook Privacy Settings:** Facebook is notorious for collecting user data, but you can limit this by managing your privacy settings. You can restrict who can see your posts, disable location tracking, and even turn off facial recognition. It's also worth reviewing which apps and websites are connected to your account and removing any you no longer use.
- **Apple Privacy Settings:** Apple offers robust privacy controls, allowing users to manage app permissions and control access to sensitive data like location, contacts, and photos. Apple's App Tracking Transparency feature ensures that apps request permission before tracking your activity across other apps and websites.

Although opting out of data collection may limit certain features, the trade-off for enhanced privacy is often worth it. Remember that some companies may continue collecting data even after opting out, so it's essential to review and update your settings.

3. **Managing App Permissions**

Mobile apps are another significant source of data collection, often accessing far more information than necessary. Carefully managing app permissions is essential to protecting your privacy and ensuring apps only access the data they need.

- **Android App Permissions:** Android devices allow you to review and adjust app permissions, giving you control over what data apps can access, such as your location, microphone, and contacts. You can grant or deny permissions for each app individually, tailoring your privacy settings to suit your needs.

- **iOS App Permissions:** IOS devices provide detailed control over app permissions. You can view which apps can access sensitive features like your location or camera and revoke access for any app that doesn't need it.

By regularly reviewing app permissions and deleting unused apps, you can minimize the amount of data mobile applications collect. This is a simple yet effective way to protect your privacy and reduce exposure to corporate surveillance.

Key Takeaways:

- **Use browser extensions to block trackers**: Install tools like Privacy Badger or uBlock Origin to stop websites from tracking you.

- **Minimize app permissions**: Grant apps only the permissions they need, such as location or contacts, and restrict unnecessary access.

- **Take control of your online ads: Platforms like Google and Facebook provide options to limit ad targeting and tracking, giving you more control over your online experience**.

- **Delete cookies regularly**: Clear your browsing data to reduce how much information websites can gather about you.

- **Use VPNs for secure browsing**: A virtual private network (VPN) encrypts your internet connection, reducing your exposure to corporate surveillance.

CHAPTER 5: GOVERNMENT OVERREACH AND YOUR PRIVACY RIGHTS

Overview: The Delicate Balance Between National Security and Personal Privacy

In today's highly digitized world, the distinction between personal privacy and government surveillance has become blurred, as the need for national security is often used to justify invasive surveillance measures. Governments worldwide argue that monitoring citizens' actions, communications, and data is necessary to protect the population from external and internal threats. However, this growing trend often comes at a steep cost—our right to personal privacy.

Understanding the intricate relationship between national security and personal privacy is essential for anyone navigating the modern digital landscape. Governments must protect their citizens from cyberattacks, terrorism, and other threats. On the other hand, excessive surveillance can erode individuals' privacy, undermining civil liberties and creating a culture of suspicion and control.

A Historical Perspective: Privacy vs. Security

The tension between privacy and security is not new; a centuries-old conflict has shaped how societies function. Throughout history, those in power have wielded surveillance to maintain control and eliminate threats. However, as technology has advanced, the methods and scope of surveillance have expanded, raising essential questions about the ethics and limits of government overreach.

The Early Days of Surveillance: Spies, Codes, and Control

Let's take a journey back to ancient times when rulers maintained their grip on power through secret networks of spies and informants. These early forms of surveillance were primitive—perhaps an intercepted message or a whispered conversation—but they laid the foundation for the modern debate on privacy versus security. The message was simple: the security of the state and the ruler's authority always took precedence over the privacy of individuals.

As centuries passed, surveillance evolved with the times. By the 20th century, technological advancements transformed surveillance into a sophisticated and organized practice. World War II was a critical turning point, as nations around the globe realized the importance of intelligence gathering. Governments developed intricate surveillance networks to monitor enemy communications, break codes, and safeguard sensitive information. Organizations such as the British MI6 and the American CIA emerged, and the balance between privacy and security shifted decisively toward the latter.

The Cold War and the Rise of Mass Surveillance

The Cold War, from the late 1940s to the early 1990s, marked an era where surveillance was no longer a tool but a full-blown strategy. During this period, espionage, wiretapping, and covert operations were the norm. Governments collected vast amounts of data, often in secret, as they sought to outmaneuver their geopolitical rivals. Privacy was scarcely a consideration, as national security was the ultimate priority.

But just as the world emerged from the shadow of the Cold War, a new revolution began—one that would change the landscape of privacy forever: the digital revolution.

The Digital Revolution: The New Battleground for Privacy

The digital revolution of the late 20th century ushered in an era of unprecedented connectivity. With the rise of the internet, smartphones, and social media, individuals began generating vast amounts of personal data. Governments quickly recognized the potential of this data and began integrating new forms of digital surveillance into their national security strategies.

However, the 9/11 terrorist attacks in 2001 marked a pivotal moment in the evolution of government surveillance. In the aftermath of the attacks, the US government passed the USA Patriot Act, granting law enforcement agencies sweeping powers to monitor communications, access personal records, and track financial transactions. The justification was clear: protecting the nation from future attacks required enhanced surveillance capabilities. However, the law raised critical questions: How much privacy are citizens willing to sacrifice for a sense of security? What are the long-term consequences of allowing governments to monitor our every move?

The Modern Era: Government Overreach and Your Privacy

In the years since 9/11, governments around the world have continued to expand their surveillance capabilities. From wiretapping and data mining to facial recognition and artificial intelligence, surveillance methods have become more sophisticated and intrusive. While many of these measures are justified as necessary for national security, there is growing concern that governments may be overstepping their bounds.

What Is Government Overreach?

Government overreach occurs when authorities exceed their legal or ethical powers, particularly concerning surveillance. While surveillance can be a valuable tool for maintaining public safety, it can also lead to the abuse of power. Programs that collect and store personal data without proper oversight or checks and balances often violate fundamental human rights, such as privacy.

Many democratic countries have laws to limit government surveillance and protect citizens' privacy. However, these laws are often outdated or inadequately enforced, leaving loopholes that allow governments to engage in surveillance practices beyond what is legally acceptable.

The Global Surveillance Landscape: A Snapshot of Big Brother in Action

The scope and intensity of government surveillance vary from country to country, but the trend toward increased citizen monitoring is evident worldwide.

In the United States, the aftermath of the 9/11 attacks saw the introduction of the Patriot Act, which granted the government the ability to conduct widespread surveillance of communications and financial records. Though it was designed to combat terrorism, the Patriot Act has been criticized for infringing on civil liberties and violating privacy rights.

Across the Atlantic, the European Union has taken a more privacy-friendly approach by introducing the General Data Protection Regulation

(GDPR). This legislation gives individuals greater control over their data and mandates that companies be transparent about collecting and using it. While GDPR is a step in the right direction, it has limitations—especially when national security concerns come into play.

Then there are countries like China, where surveillance is not just a tool but a system. The Chinese government employs extensive surveillance technologies to track and control its citizens, including facial recognition, online monitoring, and social credit systems. This surveillance infrastructure is justified to maintain order, but it has raised serious concerns about the erosion of privacy and the suppression of free speech.

Government Surveillance in the Digital Age: The New Tools of Overreach

The digital age has given governments unprecedented amounts of data about their citizens. With the help of advanced technologies such as artificial intelligence and machine learning, governments can sift through this data to identify patterns, monitor behaviors, and predict potential threats. While these tools can be used for legitimate security purposes, they can also lead to widespread surveillance and the violation of privacy rights, if not carefully regulated and monitored.

1. Artificial Intelligence: A Double-Edged Sword

Artificial intelligence (AI) has transformed how governments conduct surveillance. Machine learning algorithms can analyze vast datasets in real time, identifying patterns and anomalies impossible for human analysts to detect. This technology can help governments identify potential threats more quickly and accurately, but it also raises significant privacy concerns, particularly in the context of potential misuse and overreach.

For example, AI-powered surveillance systems can analyze data from social media, emails, phone calls, and even CCTV footage to build detailed profiles of individuals. While these profiles can be used to identify criminal behavior, they can also monitor ordinary citizens, creating a surveillance state where privacy is no longer guaranteed.

2. Facial Recognition: An Invasive Technology

Facial recognition technology is another tool that has become increasingly popular in government surveillance efforts. This technology allows governments to identify individuals in public spaces, track their movements, and monitor their activities. While facial recognition can help solve crimes and prevent attacks, it poses serious privacy risks.

Facial recognition systems are often deployed without the public's knowledge or consent. This lack of transparency has led to widespread concern that governments are using this technology to monitor citizens unlawfully.

Striking the Right Balance: Safeguarding Privacy in the Age of Surveillance

The ongoing debate over privacy versus security is one of the most critical issues of our time. While governments are responsible for protecting their citizens, they must also respect individual rights. The right balance between these competing interests requires transparency, accountability, and robust legal frameworks.

Actionable Steps for Protecting Your Privacy

As surveillance becomes more pervasive, there are steps that individuals can take to safeguard their privacy:

- **Use Encrypted Communication Tools:** Apps like Signal and WhatsApp use end-to-end encryption, making it harder for governments to monitor your messages.
- **Be Mindful of the Data You Share:** Avoid oversharing personal information on social media, and be cautious about the apps and websites you use.
- **Stay Informed:** Follow developments in privacy law and surveillance technology to understand your rights and how to protect yourself.

While the battle between privacy and security will continue to evolve, individuals must remain vigilant and proactive in protecting their personal information.

Government Surveillance Techniques: How They Work

Have you ever felt like your every digital move is being watched? That's not just paranoia—the reality is that governments worldwide are increasingly relying on advanced surveillance technologies to track online activities. So, how do they manage this? Let's dive deeply into the toolbox of modern-day government surveillance and explore the various techniques used.

- **Data Collection: The All-Seeing Eye**

Imagine that everything you do online—from browsing a news site to ordering takeout—is part of a breadcrumb trail. Governments are constantly gathering data, whether you're shopping, checking your bank balance, or sending messages. This collection isn't random or trivial; data is power. By accumulating massive amounts of information, governments can form a detailed profile of their preferences, behaviors, and future actions. The more data they collect, the more they know about you. It's as if you're under a magnifying glass, and every action is being analyzed. The result? Governments can use this data for various purposes, from national security to social control.

- **Phone and Internet Monitoring: Listening in on Your Chit-Chat**

Do you ever wonder if someone's eavesdropping on your phone conversations or peeking at your search history? Government agencies often collaborate with telecommunication companies to intercept phone calls and monitor internet traffic. This isn't limited to just occasional monitoring; they can track emails, texts, search histories, and even the websites you visit. Your entire online footprint becomes a rich source of information, almost like a detective novel unfolding chapter by chapter. Each piece of communication you make provides insights into your habits, interests, and personal connections.

In some countries, this surveillance is even more aggressive, with governments employing mass interception programs that simultaneously capture data from millions of people. Your information could still be analyzed even if you're not a target.

- **Biometric Surveillance: Face First into the Future**

Biometric data is becoming increasingly common in government surveillance efforts, with technologies like facial recognition, iris scanning, and fingerprint tracking being used at unprecedented levels. You may be familiar with these features from unlocking your smartphone, but governments are taking it much further. For instance, many airports use facial recognition to identify passengers worldwide, while high-security areas rely on iris recognition for entry control.

The power of biometrics lies in its accuracy. Unlike passwords or other forms of identification, biometrics are inherently unique to everyone, making it nearly impossible to forge or bypass. This allows governments to track people with an almost eerie precision. It's no longer just about identifying someone from a grainy photo; biometric data will enable governments to pinpoint exactly who you are, where you've been, and what you've been doing.

- **Geolocation Tracking: Where in the World Are You?**

The GPS feature on your phone is handy for finding directions, but it's also a powerful tool for tracking your every movement. Governments can use geolocation data to follow your whereabouts in real-time, whether walking to the grocery store or flying to another country. This tracking creates a comprehensive map of your daily routines, offering governments a detailed view of where you go, how long you stay, and who you might meet.

This information isn't just used for law enforcement; it can also predict behaviors, monitor political movements, and suppress dissent. In some regions, geolocation tracking has been used to monitor activists, journalists, and political opponents, leading to arrests or harassment.

- **Social Media Monitoring: What's on Your Mind?**

In the digital age, social media platforms have become integral to our lives, offering a space to share thoughts, opinions, and experiences. However, these platforms have also turned into a goldmine for government surveillance. Every status update, tweet, like, or share provides valuable data that can be used to build a detailed profile of your personal views, social circles, and political leanings.

Governments monitor social media for various reasons, from tracking terrorist activities to identifying dissenting voices. Unfortunately, this kind of surveillance can easily lead to misuse, especially in authoritarian regimes where social media posts can result in arrests or persecution. Even in democratic nations, social media monitoring can chill free expression, as people may hesitate to share their genuine opinions if they feel they're being watched.

The Impact of Government Overreach on Privacy

The increasing use of surveillance technologies poses significant risks to individual privacy. When governments collect vast amounts of data without sufficient oversight, there's a higher likelihood of that data being misused or falling into the wrong hands. Here are some of the main risks associated with government overreach:

1. Loss of Control Over Personal Data

One of the biggest concerns with mass surveillance is the lack of control individuals have over their data. Once the government collects your personal information, you have little say in how it's used, stored, or shared. This can result in sensitive data, such as medical records or financial information, accessed by parties who shouldn't have it. The lack of transparency surrounding data collection practices only worsens this issue, as citizens are often unaware of what data is being collected and why.

2. Erosion of Trust

Privacy is a cornerstone of democratic societies, and when people feel that their privacy is being violated, it can lead to a significant erosion of trust in government institutions. This is particularly true when surveillance is conducted secretly or without public oversight. Over time, this loss of confidence can undermine the very foundations of democracy, as citizens may become less likely to participate in government processes, voice their opinions, or engage in political discourse.

3. Chilling Effect on Free Speech

Surveillance doesn't just affect privacy; it also has a chilling effect on free speech. When people know their every move is being monitored, they may self-censor, avoiding controversial or critical topics of the government. This is especially true in authoritarian regimes, where surveillance is often used to suppress dissent and punish those who speak out against the ruling powers. However, even in more open societies, the fear of being watched can cause people to hold back on expressing their genuine opinions.

4. Risk of Data Breaches

Governments aren't immune to cyberattacks. The more data they collect, the greater the risk of that data being stolen in a breach. This has serious consequences, as sensitive information could be exposed to hackers, identity thieves, or foreign governments. In recent years, we've seen numerous instances where government databases have been hacked, resulting in the personal information of millions of citizens being leaked. The more data that is centralized, the bigger the target for cybercriminals.

Asserting Your Legal Rights

Even though government surveillance is widespread, individuals still have legal rights to protect their privacy. Understanding these rights is crucial to taking control of your data and resisting overreach.

- **Know Your Rights**

The first step in asserting your privacy rights is to be informed. Many countries have laws that give citizens the right to access data held by government agencies, correct inaccuracies, and request the deletion of certain types of data. These rights can vary depending on where you live, so it's essential to familiarize yourself with the privacy laws in your country.

- **Freedom of Information Laws**

In many countries, freedom of information laws allow citizens to request access to government records. For example, the Freedom of Information Act (FOIA) allows individuals to obtain documents from federal agencies in the United States. While the process can be slow and bureaucratic, these laws offer a vital tool for transparency and accountability.

- **Challenge Surveillance Programs**

In some cases, individuals and civil liberties organizations can challenge the legality of government surveillance programs. For example, in the

United States, organizations like the American Civil Liberties Union (ACLU) have filed lawsuits against mass surveillance programs, arguing that they violate constitutional rights. These legal challenges can help set essential precedents and push for reforms in surveillance practices.

Engaging in Digital Activism

Government surveillance requires collective action, and digital activism is crucial. By joining privacy advocacy groups, supporting privacy legislation, and educating others, digital activists can influence public policy and create real change.

- **Join Privacy Advocacy Groups**

Organizations like the Electronic Frontier Foundation (EFF) and Privacy International work tirelessly to protect digital rights. By joining these groups, you can stay informed and contribute to their ongoing efforts to defend privacy rights.

- **Support Privacy Legislation**

Digital activists can lobby for stronger privacy protections by supporting laws that limit government surveillance. For example, the USA Freedom Act in the United States was passed to reform aspects of the Patriot Act and curb mass surveillance. Similar legislative efforts are underway worldwide, and activism is key in pushing these reforms forward.

- **Educate Others**

Perhaps the most effective tool in the fight for privacy is education. By sharing information about government surveillance and privacy rights, digital activists can empower others to take control of their data and push for meaningful change.

Recent Government Surveillance Cases and Their Global Impact

In recent years, government surveillance programs have come under increased scrutiny, both in terms of their scale and their impact on privacy rights. Several high-profile cases and legislative actions have highlighted the growing tension between national security and personal privacy. Understanding these developments is crucial for anyone concerned with protecting their digital privacy.

1. The Edward Snowden Revelations (2013)

In 2013, Edward Snowden, a former contractor for the National Security Agency (NSA), exposed the extent of the U.S. government's surveillance programs. Snowden revealed that the NSA was collecting massive amounts of data, including phone records, emails, and internet activity from individuals worldwide. This not only raised concerns about government overreach in the U.S. but also impacted countries globally, as it became clear that foreign citizens were often caught in these surveillance nets.

Global Impact: Snowden's revelations sparked an international debate about the balance between national security and individual privacy. Many countries, including Germany, Brazil, and the United Kingdom, reevaluated their surveillance laws. The event led to the development of stricter privacy regulations, like the European Union's General Data Protection Regulation (GDPR), to protect citizens' data from government and corporate misuse.

2. China's Mass Surveillance and the Social Credit System

China has developed one of the most comprehensive surveillance systems in the world. Through its "Social Credit System," the Chinese government monitors the behavior of its citizens using a combination of facial recognition, internet activity tracking, and financial transaction monitoring. This system is designed to reward or punish citizens based on their behavior, which has raised significant concerns about human rights and individual freedoms.

Global Impact: China's surveillance model has prompted concerns that other governments might adopt similar systems to monitor and control populations. The export of Chinese surveillance technology to other countries, particularly in Africa and the Middle East, has further spread the global impact of mass surveillance. Privacy advocates worry that this could lead to a future where privacy is drastically reduced worldwide.

3. The Pegasus Spyware Scandal (2021)

In 2021, an international investigation revealed that governments around the world, including India, Hungary, Mexico, and Saudi Arabia, were using Pegasus spyware to surveil journalists, activists, and political opponents. Pegasus, developed by the Israeli firm NSO Group, allowed governments to remotely access a target's mobile phone remotely, collecting personal data and conversations and even activating the camera and microphone without the user's knowledge.

Global Impact: The Pegasus scandal demonstrated the broad reach of government surveillance and how easily it could infringe on individual privacy rights. Governments and human rights organizations worldwide condemned the abuse of surveillance technology, leading to calls for stricter regulation of spyware and increased protections for journalists and activists.

4. Surveillance in the United Kingdom: The Investigatory Powers Act (2016)

Often referred to as the "Snooper's Charter," the UK's Investigatory Powers Act of 2016 gave the government sweeping powers to conduct mass surveillance. It allows law enforcement and intelligence agencies to collect communications data, including internet activity and phone calls, without a warrant. Critics argue that the act undermines civil liberties and fails to protect personal data adequately.

Global Impact: The Investigatory Powers Act sparked widespread concern across Europe and influenced the debate about data privacy and government power. While the UK defends the law as necessary for national security, it has set a precedent that other countries may follow, risking the normalization of mass surveillance in democratic nations.

5. The U.S. Foreign Intelligence Surveillance Act (FISA) and PRISM Program

The U.S. government's PRISM program, authorized under the Foreign Intelligence Surveillance Act (FISA), allows intelligence agencies to collect data from major technology companies, such as Google, Facebook, and Microsoft, under the guise of national security. This has raised significant concerns about how much private information is accessible to the government without individuals' consent or knowledge.

Global Impact: PRISM exposed the level of collaboration between government agencies and tech giants, raising international concerns about how corporations handle user data. The program has also led to increased encryption efforts by technology companies to reassure users that their data is safe from government surveillance.

The Global Pushback Against Surveillance

In response to these cases, there has been a growing movement advocating for stronger privacy laws and more oversight of government surveillance programs. Privacy advocates, international organizations, and governments alike are increasingly focused on curbing the misuse of surveillance tools and ensuring that citizens' privacy rights are respected.

- **General Data Protection Regulation (GDPR)**: One of the most comprehensive data privacy laws in the world, the GDPR has set a global standard for data protection, forcing companies and governments to be more transparent about how they collect and use personal data.

- **Evolving Legal Protections**: Countries like Brazil, India, and Australia have implemented or are developing their own data privacy laws inspired by the GDPR. These laws aim to give citizens more control over their data and limit the scope of government surveillance.

Key Takeaways:

- **Use encrypted messaging apps**: Communicate securely with tools like Signal or WhatsApp, which offer end-to-end encryption.

- **Learn your legal rights**: Understand the privacy laws in your region and how they protect you from government surveillance.

- **Use a VPN**: A VPN can hide your IP address and online activities from government monitoring.

- **Engage in digital activism**: Support organizations fighting for digital privacy and transparency, such as the Electronic Frontier Foundation (EFF).

- **Empower yourself: Be mindful of the data you share on public platforms. By limiting your digital footprint, you can take control and** reduce the risk of surveillance.

CHAPTER 6: THE ROLE OF ARTIFICIAL INTELLIGENCE IN PRIVACY

Overview: AI-Driven Surveillance and Data Protection Tools

Artificial Intelligence (AI) has emerged as one of the most powerful tools in the modern world, shaping how personal information is collected, analyzed, and protected. Its role in surveillance is groundbreaking and controversial, as it allows for unprecedented data collection and analysis, which can be both beneficial and invasive. Simultaneously, AI is also being leveraged to develop sophisticated tools to protect user privacy and secure sensitive information. The delicate balance between AI as a tool for surveillance and its role in safeguarding privacy defines the current privacy landscape.

AI-Driven Surveillance: A Revolutionary, Yet Invasive Technology

Surveillance, traditionally the domain of governments and security agencies, has been transformed by AI into a complex web of data tracking, behavioral monitoring, and predictive analysis. AI-driven surveillance technologies can process vast data at unimaginable speeds, turning raw information into actionable insights for corporations, governments, and other organizations.

One of the key features of AI surveillance is its ability to "learn" from the data it collects. Machine learning algorithms, a core component of AI, enable systems to continuously refine and improve their accuracy by analyzing trends and patterns within the data. Allows AI-driven surveillance systems to become more efficient over time, leading to more precise targeting of individuals and behaviors. For example, predictive policing uses AI algorithms to analyze historical crime data, allowing law enforcement to anticipate where crimes may occur. It sounds like a step forward for safety, but it also raises ethical concerns about discrimination and potential abuse.

At the heart of this transformation is using biometric data—personal identifiers like fingerprints, facial recognition, and voice patterns. AI can analyze and cross-reference these unique identifiers to track individuals across various platforms and locations. Facial recognition technology, mainly, has seen widespread adoption across airports, public spaces, and retail environments. While this offers significant security and customer personalization benefits, it also means that individuals can be constantly monitored without explicit consent. The invasive nature of such surveillance raises deep concerns about individual freedoms and privacy rights.

Moreover, location tracking powered by AI is now integrated into almost every smartphone and wearable device. AI algorithms utilize GPS, Wi-Fi signals, and other location data to monitor real-time individual movements. These insights are often shared with third-party advertisers and corporations, allowing them to target users with personalized content and ads based on where they've been, what they've purchased, or even who they've interacted with.

AI surveillance systems are not limited to physical spaces. Online platforms are also hotspots for AI-driven data collection. Social media platforms, e-commerce sites, and search engines use AI to analyze user behaviors, preferences, and interactions to create personalized experiences. These platforms track user data across multiple devices, building detailed profiles that can be used for targeted advertising, content recommendations, or, in some cases, political influence. A well-known example is the **Cambridge Analytica scandal**, where AI and data-driven strategies were used to target and influence voters during major political campaigns.

While the capabilities of AI-driven surveillance continue to expand, they bring profound implications for privacy, autonomy, and freedom. The challenge lies in finding a balance between leveraging AI for legitimate purposes like security and innovation and ensuring that individual rights to privacy are not violated.

The Rise of AI in Corporate Surveillance

Corporations, especially those in the technology sector, are the most significant users of AI for surveillance purposes. Social media platforms like Facebook, Twitter, and Instagram employ sophisticated AI algorithms to track user behavior, engagement patterns, and emotional states. These companies use AI to analyze posts, comments, likes, shares, and other interactions, creating a rich data profile that can be monetized through targeted advertising.

Furthermore, e-commerce giants like Amazon and Alibaba use AI to predict consumer behavior. By analyzing past purchases, search queries, and browsing history, AI helps these platforms predict what customers will likely buy next, which products they will show interest in, and even the price point they may accept. While this has revolutionized the convenience and personalization of online shopping, it also means that users are being monitored at every step of their digital journey.

The most concerning aspect of corporate AI surveillance is the monetization of personal data. AI-driven systems allow companies to sell user data to third-party advertisers, data brokers, and even governments. The data collected—often without the user's clear understanding or consent—fuels a multi-billion-dollar industry where personal information is commoditized. This raises ethical questions about the ownership of personal data and individuals' rights over how their data is used. While companies often claim that this data collection is benign and done for the sake of "improving user experience," the fact remains that personal privacy is being sacrificed for profit.

In addition, emotional surveillance is an emerging frontier in corporate AI usage. Companies are experimenting with AI tools that can detect emotional states based on facial expressions, voice tone, and even typing patterns. These AI-driven technologies are being used in marketing to determine how users react to specific advertisements or products, allowing companies to tailor their approaches in real time. The implications of emotional surveillance are staggering as companies gain the ability to manipulate users' emotions, influence their decisions, and potentially even control their moods through targeted content.

AI as a Tool for Privacy Protection

Conversely, AI is also being used to develop advanced privacy protection tools that empower individuals to safeguard their data. These tools help users manage, protect, and minimize their digital footprint in an increasingly data-driven world.

AI-powered encryption is one such tool. Traditionally, encryption methods relied on static algorithms to encode and protect data. Today, AI-driven encryption is dynamic and adaptive, using machine learning to detect potential threats and adjust encryption protocols in real-time. AI can anticipate attacks, like attempts to intercept data during transmission, and automatically strengthen the encryption algorithms to protect the data. AI-powered encryption is beneficial in industries where sensitive data—such as financial records, health information, or personal identities—must be protected at all costs.

Anonymization is another AI-powered technique that has revolutionized data privacy. AI-driven anonymization tools allow companies to use data for analysis without compromising individual identities. These tools use algorithms to strip personal identifiers from data sets, replacing them with pseudo-randomized information. This ensures that companies can still gain insights from the data but cannot trace it back to any particular individual. AI-powered anonymization is used by companies like Google and Apple, which collect massive amounts of user data but ensure that none of it can be linked directly to an individual.

Additionally, **AI-powered personal data audits** are becoming increasingly accessible to individuals. These audits use AI to analyze a person's online presence, identify where their data is stored, and provide recommendations on securing or deleting it. For example, AI can track down old accounts that a user may have forgotten, identify websites that hold their personal information, and suggest steps to reduce their digital footprint. These audits empower individuals to take control of their data and privacy in ways that were previously difficult or impossible to achieve.

The Paradox of AI in Privacy: A Tool for Both Good and Harm

The duality of AI's role in privacy highlights a paradox: the same technology that invades privacy can also protect it. AI surveillance tools can intrude on every aspect of a person's life, from monitoring online activities to tracking physical movements. Yet, AI is also critical for developing tools to safeguard against these intrusions.

For instance, AI is central to developing **privacy-preserving machine learning**—a branch of AI that enables algorithms to learn from data without directly accessing it. In privacy-preserving machine learning, AI models can be trained using encrypted data, ensuring that sensitive information is never exposed during training. This approach is critical in sectors like healthcare, where patient data must be kept confidential. However, it can still be used to train AI models for medical research and treatment innovations.

At the same time, the very presence of AI in privacy raises critical ethical considerations. How much data is too much? Where do we draw the line between beneficial surveillance and harmful intrusion? As AI continues to evolve, these questions become more pressing. Governments and regulatory bodies are already beginning to grapple with AI's implications for privacy, with new laws and regulations being drafted to address these concerns. However, keeping up with the rapid pace of AI development will be a constant challenge.

Actionable Solutions: Using AI-Powered Privacy Tools

In the evolving digital privacy landscape, AI can be harnessed as a powerful tool to shield personal data from prying eyes. While the same technology that drives surveillance can be used to track and monitor user activity, it can also provide sophisticated solutions to protect individual privacy. The key lies in using AI tools effectively to balance convenience with security. Here are several AI-powered privacy solutions that can be implemented to protect and manage your data.

1. Differential Privacy: Safeguarding Personal Data through AI

Differential privacy is a concept that has gained momentum in recent years due to its ability to protect individual privacy while still allowing organizations to glean insights from large data sets. AI plays a critical role in enabling differential privacy by adding statistical noise to data, thus obscuring individual entries while maintaining the integrity of the overall dataset. This method ensures that even if data is shared or analyzed, personal information cannot be traced back to any specific individual.

For instance, companies like Apple and Google have adopted differential privacy in their data collection strategies. AI algorithms introduce random variations into the data collected, ensuring that the specific details of an individual user's interactions remain private. This method allows these companies to study user behavior patterns without compromising user privacy.

In practical terms, differential privacy can be applied to various aspects of your digital life. For example, when using an AI-powered platform that collects behavioral data—whether for personalized recommendations or performance analytics—the system can anonymize your inputs to ensure your data remains private. As more platforms integrate AI to enhance their services, understanding how differential privacy works can empower individuals to engage with technology more securely.

2. Privacy-Centric Artificial Intelligence: AI's Role in Decentralized Systems

A growing trend in privacy technology is the shift toward decentralized systems, where data ownership remains with the user rather than stored in centralized servers. AI enhances these systems by offering decentralized privacy protection methods, such as federated learning, which enables AI models to train on decentralized data without sharing personal information.

Federated learning allows AI systems to improve algorithms using data from multiple devices without centralizing that data. For instance, a smartphone using AI-driven predictive text can enhance functionality by learning from the user's typing patterns. Still, the data remains on the device rather than being sent to a central server. This ensures the user retains control over their data while benefiting from AI-driven features.

Decentralized privacy systems using AI are particularly effective in environments where sensitive information—such as financial data, healthcare records, or personal communications—is at risk. By keeping data decentralized, individuals reduce their exposure to potential data breaches or unauthorized access.

3. AI-Based Privacy Audits: Tracking and Managing Digital Footprints

One of the challenges in protecting digital privacy is the sheer amount of data individuals generate and share daily. Keeping track of what data is being shared, with whom, and for what purpose can be overwhelming. AI-powered privacy audit tools can automatically scan an individual's digital footprint, providing a comprehensive report on where their data is stored, who has access to it, and how it is used.

For example, tools like *Jumbo* and *Mine* utilize AI to perform privacy audits by scanning your social media accounts, email, and online services to identify which platforms can access your data. These tools then provide actionable recommendations on reclaiming control over that data—whether through deleting unused accounts, revoking permissions, or adjusting privacy settings.

AI-based privacy audit tools can also provide insights into potential vulnerabilities, such as accounts with weak passwords or excessive permissions granted to third-party apps. By automating the privacy audit process, AI tools can save individuals time while protecting their personal information.

4. AI-Powered Encryption: Securing Data in Transit and at rest

Encryption is the cornerstone of digital security, and AI is revolutionizing how encryption is applied and managed. While effective, traditional encryption methods often require manual implementation and updates, leaving room for human error. AI-powered encryption, however, automates this process, ensuring that data is always protected without constant user intervention.

One example is AI-driven dynamic encryption, where the system automatically adapts encryption protocols based on the sensitivity of the data and the threat landscape. AI algorithms can detect changes in the environment—such as a shift from a secure to an insecure network—and respond instantly by adjusting encryption levels or triggering alerts. This ensures that personal data, whether in transit or at rest, is always protected under optimal conditions.

Moreover, AI-powered encryption systems can detect and respond to potential breaches faster than traditional methods. For instance, in cases where malicious actors attempt to intercept encrypted data, AI can analyze real-time threat patterns and adjust encryption protocols or isolate compromised systems, thereby reducing the risk of data theft.

5. Smart Privacy Assistants: Personal AI Guardians

Intelligent privacy assistants are another innovative solution powered by AI. These virtual assistants monitor your digital activity in real-time, providing recommendations on privacy settings, warning of potential threats, and automatically adjusting settings to enhance privacy. Like how virtual assistants like Siri or Google Assistant help users with tasks, privacy assistants act as guardians over personal data.

For instance, privacy assistants like *PrivacyFix* or *Guardio* analyze the permissions granted to apps and services on your devices and recommend changes based on privacy concerns. They can suggest disabling tracking features, restricting access to sensitive information like location data, and alerting users to unusual or potentially harmful behaviors by third-party apps.

Privacy assistants also learn from user behaviors to offer increasingly personalized recommendations. Over time, these assistants can anticipate the user's needs and proactively adjust security settings, reducing the risk of data exposure without requiring continuous user input. This personalized and adaptive approach is one of the critical advantages of

AI-powered privacy solutions, making it easier for individuals to maintain solid digital privacy.

6. Anonymizing Data Through AI-Enhanced Tools

Data anonymization is essential for ensuring privacy, particularly when sharing or storing large volumes of information. AI tools enhance anonymization techniques by identifying patterns in data that may unintentionally reveal personal information and then taking steps to obscure or modify that data to ensure privacy.

An example of this is the use of AI in medical research. When healthcare organizations share patient data for research purposes, AI algorithms can anonymize the data by removing identifiable information while retaining the integrity of the dataset. This ensures that researchers can access the data without compromising patient privacy.

Additionally, AI can dynamically assess whether anonymization remains effective over time. As technology evolves, anonymization techniques can become outdated or ineffective against emerging threats. AI systems can automatically update and enhance anonymization protocols, ensuring long-term privacy protection.

7. AI-Powered Anti-Tracking Tools: Blocking Digital Footprints

AI is also leading the development of advanced anti-tracking tools that prevent websites, advertisers, and third parties from tracking user behavior across the Internet. AI powers anti-tracking tools such as Privacy Badger and Ghostery to identify and block trackers in real-time, ensuring that individuals' online activities remain private.

What sets AI-powered anti-tracking tools apart is their ability to learn from new tracking methods and adapt accordingly. As advertisers and websites develop more sophisticated ways to track users—through browser fingerprinting or cross-device tracking—AI algorithms can detect these new techniques and block them before they compromise privacy.

These tools prevent unwanted tracking, improve browsing speed, and reduce the amount of personal data collected by advertisers. By using AI to stay ahead of evolving tracking techniques, individuals can browse the internet confidently, knowing that their data is not being harvested without consent.

8. AI in Data Minimization: Reducing exposure

Another critical privacy solution powered by AI is data minimization. This principle states that only the necessary amount of data should be collected, processed, and stored, reducing exposure risk. AI can automatically assess the relevance of data and minimize the amount collected to what is strictly needed for a particular purpose.

For example, AI-driven services can analyze user data requests and reject any that exceed the minimum requirements. This is particularly important in healthcare, finance, and e-commerce industries, where large amounts of personal data are often requested. By using AI to minimize data collection, organizations can reduce the risk of data breaches and ensure that personal information is only stored for as long as necessary.

In addition, AI-based systems can enforce data retention policies by automatically deleting data that is no longer needed, further protecting individuals from potential privacy violations.

Managing AI Recommendations

AI is now ubiquitous in recommendation systems, from suggesting what movies to watch on streaming platforms to what products to buy online. These recommendation systems are powered by AI algorithms that analyze user behavior and preferences to provide personalized suggestions. While this can improve user experiences, it also raises privacy concerns.

The Hidden Dangers of Recommendation Systems

AI-powered recommendation systems rely on extensive data collection to function effectively. Data is collected, processed, and stored every time a user interacts with a recommendation system, whether on social media, shopping platforms, or content streaming services. This data is then used to make future recommendations, creating a continuous feedback loop that further entrenches AI-driven data collection.

One of the hidden dangers of AI recommendations is that they often contribute to creating "filter bubbles." A filter bubble is a situation where the information presented to an individual is tailored to their beliefs, interests, or preferences, limiting their exposure to diverse perspectives. AI recommendation systems can create echo chambers by only showing users content that aligns with their previous behaviors and interests, which can have long-term societal consequences, including polarization and misinformation.

Moreover, recommendation systems often require the collection of personal data to operate effectively, and this data is typically collected without the user's explicit consent. Many users are unaware that their browsing history, search queries, and even location data are being used to generate these recommendations.

How to Manage AI Recommendations for Better Privacy

Managing AI recommendations can be challenging, but there are actionable steps individuals can take to protect their privacy while still benefiting from these systems.

1. **Limit Data Sharing**: Many platforms allow users to limit the data they share with recommendation systems. For example, users can turn off tracking features, limit the amount of personal data shared with third-party services, or turn off personalized advertising.

2. **Use Privacy-Focused Platforms**: Some platforms are designed with user privacy in mind, offering alternative approaches to recommendation systems. For example, DuckDuckGo is a search engine that doesn't track user activity, so it doesn't generate personalized recommendations based on browsing history.

3. **Regularly Clear Data**: Many platforms store user data to improve the accuracy of their recommendation systems. Users can manage their data privacy by regularly clearing browsing history, cookies, and other stored data that recommendation systems rely on. Some platforms also offer settings that allow users to clear their recommendation history, resetting the system's understanding of their preferences.

4. **Adjust Privacy Settings**: Social media platforms, content streaming services, and online marketplaces offer privacy settings that can be adjusted to limit the data used for recommendations.

For instance, on Facebook, users can control how their activity is used to personalize ads and content suggestions.

Controlling Targeted Advertising

Targeted advertising is one of the most pervasive uses of AI in the digital landscape. Advertisers use AI algorithms to analyze user behavior and deliver personalized ads based on interests, browsing history, and online interactions. While targeted ads can improve relevance and reduce ad fatigue, they pose significant privacy risks.

How AI Powers Targeted Advertising

AI-driven advertising platforms like Google Ads and Facebook Ads use machine learning algorithms to collect and analyze user data from various sources. This data is then used to segment users into specific groups based on their demographics, interests, and behaviors. Once segmented, advertisers can create personalized ad campaigns targeting particular user groups, increasing engagement and conversion rates.

The problem with targeted advertising is that it often involves collecting large amounts of personal data without the user's knowledge. Advertisers sometimes use data brokers to acquire additional information about users, including offline behaviors, such as purchasing habits, that can be combined with online data to create even more detailed profiles.

Mitigating the Risks of Targeted Advertising

Controlling targeted advertising is essential for maintaining digital privacy. There are several ways individuals can mitigate the risks associated with AI-powered advertising:

1. **Opt Out of Targeted Ads**: Many platforms allow users to opt out of targeted ads. For example, Google and Facebook offer settings where users can turn off ad personalization, preventing the platform from using their browsing history and personal data to deliver targeted ads.

2. **Use Ad Blockers**: Privacy-focused browser extensions like uBlock Origin and Privacy Badger can block ads and trackers, preventing advertisers from collecting data on user behavior. These tools can be particularly effective at reducing exposure to targeted ads.

3. **Limit Data Collection**: By limiting the data collected by social media platforms, search engines, and other online services, users can reduce the amount of information available to advertisers. Adjusting privacy settings to turn off data tracking, location sharing, and third-party data sharing is crucial in controlling targeted advertising.

4. **Use Privacy-Focused Search Engines**: Search engines like DuckDuckGo and Start page don't track user behavior or store personal data, making them ideal for individuals looking to avoid targeted ads. Using these platforms, users can reduce the likelihood of their data being used for advertising.

Actionable Steps:

- **Understand AI-driven privacy risks**: Be aware of how AI tools, such as facial recognition and behavioral tracking, collect and analyze personal data.

- **Use AI-driven privacy tools**: Leverage AI-powered privacy tools, such as those that help manage your digital footprint or block intrusive tracking.

- **Regularly audit AI-powered services**: Evaluate the AI-driven services you use and understand their data collection policies.

- **Control AI personalization settings**: In AI-driven platforms, manage settings to reduce the amount of data used for personalization and targeting.

- **Stay informed about AI privacy laws**: Follow developments in AI regulation and how they impact your privacy.

BIOMETRIC DATA
THE NEW FRONTIER

CHAPTER 7: BIOMETRIC DATA – THE NEW FRONTIER

In today's world, technology has evolved to a point where our very biology is used to verify our identity. Biometric data—information derived from unique physical traits such as fingerprints, facial features, voice patterns, and even iris scans—has become a cornerstone of modern security systems. While biometrics offer undeniable convenience, they also raise significant concerns about privacy and the potential misuse of personal data. This chapter will explore the rise of biometric data in security, its implications for privacy, and actionable steps individuals and organizations can take to manage their biometric information responsibly.

Overview: The rise of biometric data in security and its privacy implications.

In a world where technology touches every corner of our lives, using biometric data for security has evolved into a transformative tool. Biometric systems, which rely on unique physiological or behavioral characteristics to verify identity, have come to play a pivotal role in enhancing the efficiency and security of authentication processes across various sectors. While this advancement promises unprecedented levels of convenience, its growing presence has stirred significant concerns regarding the privacy of individuals, raising a critical question: How do we balance the benefits of biometrics with the inherent risks to personal privacy?

A Shift from Passwords to Biometrics

Historically, security systems relied on traditional authentication methods such as passwords and PINs to protect personal information. However, these methods are fraught with vulnerabilities. While widely used, passwords are often weak, reused across multiple platforms, and easily compromised through social engineering attacks, brute force attempts, or data breaches. The surge in cyberattacks has exposed the limitations of such systems, pushing security innovators to seek more robust, more reliable alternatives.

Once confined to science fiction, biometric technology quickly emerged as a solution. By utilizing intrinsic characteristics unique to each person, such as fingerprints, retina patterns, or voice recognition, biometric systems offer a more robust layer of protection. Unlike passwords that can be forgotten or stolen, biometric data provides a seamless, secure, and fast method for authentication. Today, many devices, including smartphones and banking systems, rely on biometrics to authenticate users, replacing the need for typed passwords.

However, as the use of biometric data has expanded, so have the questions about its safety and privacy implications. While it is true that biometric systems are more challenging to crack, the fact that biometric data is intimately tied to an individual's physical identity brings about profound challenges that must be addressed.

Convenience with Consequences

The allure of biometric security lies mainly in its convenience. Unlocking a smartphone with a fingerprint or paying using facial recognition saves time and effort. Biometrics have become indispensable in industries where speed and efficiency are paramount, such as banking, healthcare, and even retail. Airports, for instance, have adopted facial recognition systems to expedite identity verification, while hospitals increasingly use biometric scanners to safeguard patient data.

However, convenience often comes at the expense of privacy. Unlike passwords, which can be updated regularly, biometric data is permanent. A compromised password can be changed within minutes. Still, the theft of biometric data such as a fingerprint or facial scan presents a greater risk, as these identifiers cannot be altered. If this information falls into the wrong hands, the consequences can be long-lasting and difficult to mitigate.

Moreover, because biometric data is often stored in centralized databases, it becomes an attractive target for cybercriminals. A breach of such a database not only exposes the personal information of millions but also presents a significant threat to an individual's identity security. The risk of identity theft or fraud increases exponentially when biometric data is involved, as it is much harder to repudiate or rectify.

Ethical Concerns and Corporate Responsibility

New ethical concerns arise as businesses and governments adopt biometric technologies on a larger scale. Corporations and institutions gather vast amounts of personal information, often without providing full transparency regarding how this data is stored, used, or shared. Sometimes, individuals may be unaware that their biometric data is being collected. For example, companies may implement facial recognition systems in public spaces, gathering information without obtaining explicit consent from those monitored.

This raises significant privacy concerns regarding how third parties handle biometric data. Corporations may sometimes share or sell biometric information to advertisers or government agencies, opening the door to unauthorized use or surveillance. Such practices erode the public's trust in corporations and governments, highlighting the need for greater transparency and regulatory oversight.

Ethical dilemmas also emerge when considering the use of biometrics for targeted surveillance. Governments worldwide have increasingly turned to facial recognition and other biometric technologies to monitor public spaces, identify criminals, and enhance national security. While such measures can be effective in preventing crime, they also have the potential to infringe upon civil liberties and enable mass surveillance. The misuse of biometric data by authoritarian regimes, for example, can lead to the tracking and persecution of political dissidents or minority groups, amplifying concerns about human rights violations.

The Challenge of Data Security

One of the most significant implications of the rise of biometric data is the challenge of securing this susceptible information. Traditional data breaches involving usernames or passwords are serious, but the implications of a breach involving biometric data are far more severe. Once biometric data is stolen, it cannot be replaced, making securing these systems a top priority for organizations that handle such information.

Biometric systems require vast amounts of data storage and processing power, which increases the risk of vulnerabilities. Additionally, since biometric authentication often occurs on personal devices like smartphones, the risk of theft or loss is ever-present. When biometric data is stored locally on a device, it may be protected by security measures. Still, when it is transmitted to a centralized system for verification, the data becomes vulnerable to interception or hacking. A breach in such a system could result in the permanent exposure of sensitive biometric information.

Many organizations lack robust data protection practices, compounding the challenge of securing biometric data. Companies sometimes fail to encrypt or anonymize biometric data properly, leaving it vulnerable to theft. As biometric technologies continue to evolve, organizations need to implement comprehensive data security measures to ensure the safe storage and transmission of biometric information. This includes using encryption, tokenization, and decentralized storage solutions that minimize the risk of data breaches.

Implications for Individuals and Society

The rise of biometric technology has far-reaching implications, not only for individuals but for society as a whole. On an individual level, biometric data offers enhanced security and convenience but also exposes people to new risks. Beyond identity theft, there is also the potential for discrimination based on biometric data. For example, facial recognition systems have been shown to have higher error rates when identifying individuals with darker skin tones, raising concerns about bias and fairness in using this technology.

On a broader societal level, the widespread adoption of biometric systems raises important questions about privacy, surveillance, and the role of technology in shaping our lives. As biometric data becomes increasingly integrated into everyday activities, from making purchases to boarding flights, individuals may feel they are losing control over their personal information. This sense of helplessness can erode trust in institutions and lead to a growing demand for stronger privacy protections.

Governments and regulatory bodies must establish clear guidelines for the use and protection of biometric data. This includes implementing strict consent requirements, ensuring that biometric data is collected and used transparently, and holding organizations accountable for breaches or misuse of such data. Without proper regulation, the rise of biometric technology could lead to an erosion of privacy rights and the normalization of mass surveillance.

The Future of Biometric Privacy

As biometric data continues to shape the future of security, society must carefully weigh the benefits of this technology against its potential threats to privacy. While biometrics undoubtedly offer a more secure and efficient method of authentication, the risks associated with their misuse cannot be ignored. Moving forward, governments, corporations, and individuals need to work together to create a framework that safeguards biometric data while still allowing for the advancement of this powerful technology.

Innovative solutions, such as decentralized biometric storage and advanced encryption techniques, may be vital in addressing the privacy concerns associated with biometrics. Public awareness and education are also crucial for empowering individuals to make informed decisions about when and how to share their biometric data.

Ultimately, the rise of biometric data represents both an opportunity and a challenge. If handled responsibly, biometric technology can offer unparalleled security benefits while respecting individuals' privacy. However, without proper oversight and protections, the widespread use of biometrics could pose a significant threat to our fundamental right to privacy. The task before us is to navigate this complex landscape cautiously, ensuring that the future of biometric technology upholds the highest privacy and security standards for all.

Actionable Solutions: Manage biometric data storage and usage and stay informed about biometric data laws.

The unique nature of biometric data demands stringent management practices to prevent misuse or exploitation. Since biometrics are permanent, unlike passwords, the consequences of a data breach involving biometric information are far-reaching. To minimize the risks, individuals and organizations must adopt meticulous strategies to safeguard biometric data and ensure its responsible use.

1. Implementing Strong Encryption Protocols

Encryption is the backbone of data security. Just as passwords and other sensitive information are encrypted, biometric data should be subjected to the highest levels of encryption. When biometric data is stored—whether on a device or in the cloud—it must be encrypted so that even if it is intercepted, it cannot be accessed or used maliciously.

Organizations handling biometric data should invest in advanced encryption algorithms such as AES-256, a widely respected encryption standard known for its robustness. Encryption should also be applied during storage and the transmission of biometric data, such as when it's sent from a device to a server.

Individuals must ensure that their services and devices employ proper encryption techniques. Many biometric-enabled devices store this data locally, which is a safer option than sending it to a cloud database. However, checking whether the data is encrypted locally and ensuring regular updates are applied to these devices will further enhance security.

2. Local vs. Cloud-Based Storage of Biometric Data

A critical decision for managing biometric data storage is to store it locally (on a device) or in the cloud (on remote servers). Each method has its own set of advantages and risks.

- **Local Storage**: Many modern smartphones, for example, use local storage to house biometric data. Apple's Face ID and Touch ID store facial recognition and fingerprint data directly on the device within a secure enclave, ensuring that the data never leaves the device. This provides a significant advantage in terms of security because even if the company's cloud servers are hacked, the biometric data remains secure. Local storage is often more secure because it minimizes exposure to external threats.

- **Cloud-Based Storage**: Some services and organizations opt for cloud-based storage, which allows them to manage large amounts of data centrally. While cloud storage can improve accessibility and scalability, it also increases the risk of mass data breaches. Storing biometric data in the cloud means it can be vulnerable to cyberattacks, notably if the cloud provider lacks robust security protocols. For this reason, individuals and companies need to carefully vet cloud storage providers, ensuring that they offer top-notch security measures, such as encryption, multi-factor authentication, and regular security audits.

Individuals should opt for services that offer local storage options for biometric data whenever possible. Companies handling sensitive biometric information should prioritize local storage for users to mitigate the risks of large-scale breaches.

3. Using Multi-Factor Authentication (MFA) with Biometric Data

Multi-factor authentication (MFA) has become a standard for securing accounts, and its integration with biometric data can further enhance security. Instead of relying solely on biometric authentication, MFA adds an extra layer of protection, requiring users to provide additional credentials such as a password or a one-time code. This approach significantly reduces the risk of unauthorized access, even if biometric data is compromised.

For instance, many mobile banking apps allow users to log in using facial recognition or fingerprints but also require a PIN or password for high-risk activities like transferring funds. This method ensures that attackers still need the additional authentication factor to gain access even if biometric data is somehow intercepted.

Both individuals and organizations should adopt MFA for systems using biometric authentication. This will ensure greater security and build trust with users by demonstrating that privacy and protection are top priorities.

4. Regularly Reviewing and Updating Biometric Data Policies

For organizations, managing biometric data effectively requires regular reviews of internal policies. Technology evolves rapidly, and the tools used to protect biometric information must grow alongside it. Companies should establish clear guidelines for collecting, storing, and using biometric data, with regular audits to ensure compliance with the latest security standards.

<u>Biometric data policies should address the following key areas:</u>

- **Data Minimization**: Collect only the biometric data necessary for the intended purpose. Avoid excessive data collection that could expose individuals to more significant risks.

- **Access Control**: Limit access to biometric data to only those who need it. Implement role-based access controls (RBAC) and ensure employees handling biometric data are trained in data security practices.

- **Retention and Deletion Policies**: Define how long biometric data will be stored and establish clear guidelines for safely deleting it once it is no longer needed. Retaining biometric data longer than necessary increases the risk of breaches.

- **Transparency**: Communicate to users how their biometric data is collected, stored, and used. Transparency fosters trust and ensures compliance with data protection regulations.

Individuals should periodically review the privacy policies of the services they use, especially those involving biometric data. Pay attention to updates in terms of service that may change how your biometric data is handled.

5. **Educating Employees and Users About Biometric Data Security**

Awareness is a crucial element in safeguarding biometric data. Organizations should regularly train employees who manage or interact with biometric systems. The training should cover best practices for handling sensitive data, recognizing potential threats (like phishing attempts), and understanding the legal implications of mismanaging biometric information.

Users must also stay informed about the security measures in place for their biometric services. This includes understanding how to turn biometric authentication on or off devices, set up MFA, and recognize when additional security steps may be needed.

Staying Informed About Biometric Data Laws

As biometric data becomes increasingly integrated into daily life, the legal frameworks governing its use continue to evolve. Staying informed about biometric data laws is essential for individuals and organizations to ensure compliance and safeguard privacy. Biometric data laws vary by region, with some countries and states offering more robust protections than others. Below are several key aspects to consider when staying informed about biometric data laws.

1. **Understanding Regional Variations in Biometric Data Regulations**

Biometric data laws are not uniform globally, and understanding the regional variations is crucial for ensuring compliance. Some jurisdictions have implemented strict biometric data regulations, while others may still be in the early stages of creating legal frameworks.

For example, in the United States, Illinois has been at the forefront of biometric privacy laws with the **Biometric Information Privacy Act (BIPA)**. BIPA requires companies to obtain explicit consent before collecting biometric data and allows individuals to sue for violations. It also mandates that companies establish retention schedules for biometric data and delete it once it is no longer needed.

In contrast, other states, such as California and Texas, have passed their versions of biometric privacy laws, though they differ in scope and enforcement. Outside the U.S., the **General Data Protection Regulation (GDPR)** in the European Union classifies biometric data as a "special category" of personal data, subjecting it to stringent consent and security requirements.

Staying informed about these regional differences is vital for organizations operating in multiple locations. Failure to comply with local biometric data laws can result in fines and legal consequences. Individuals should also be aware of their rights under local regulations, as some jurisdictions provide avenues for redress if biometric data is mishandled.

2. **Consent and Transparency: The Foundation of Biometric Data Laws**

One of the core principles of biometric data laws is the requirement for informed consent. Most biometric data regulations, such as BIPA and GDPR, require companies to obtain explicit consent before collecting or processing biometric data. This means that individuals must be fully informed about what data is being collected, how it will be used, and how long it will be stored.

Another critical requirement is transparency. Organizations must be transparent about how biometric data will be used, who will have access to it, and whether it will be shared with third parties. This level of transparency builds trust with users and ensures compliance with data protection regulations.

Individuals need to read and understand privacy policies related to biometric data. Before consenting to collect biometric information, ensure you are comfortable with how your data will be used and whether the company has adequate security measures in place.

3. **The Role of Regulatory Bodies and Enforcement**

Regulatory bodies such as the **Federal Trade Commission (FTC)** in the U.S. and **Data Protection Authorities (DPAs)** in the EU play a critical role in enforcement to ensure that biometric data laws are followed. These agencies investigate violations of biometric data laws, issue fines, and guide companies on how to comply with regulations.

For example, under GDPR, DPA can impose fines of up to 4% of a company's global annual revenue for severe violations involving biometric data. Similarly, the FTC can act against companies in the U.S. that mislead consumers about their use of biometric data.

Organizations need to stay up to date with regulatory bodies' guidance and ensure that their practices align with the latest legal requirements. Individuals can also turn to these agencies if they believe their biometric data has been mishandled or want to learn more about their rights.

4. Preparing for Future Biometric Data Legislation

The legal landscape surrounding biometric data constantly evolves, and more comprehensive laws are expected soon. Governments worldwide recognize the need to regulate biometric data more strictly as its usage becomes more widespread.

To prepare for future legislation, organizations should adopt a proactive approach to data management by:

- **Implementing Privacy by Design**: This approach involves integrating privacy considerations into every biometric data collection and processing stage. By designing systems with privacy in mind, companies can ensure compliance with future laws and regulations.

- **Staying Informed**: It is critical to keep up with legal developments and regulatory trends. Companies should monitor proposed legislation, industry best practices, and enforcement actions to anticipate changes that may impact their biometric data policies.

- **Engaging Legal Counsel**: Consulting with legal experts specializing in data protection and privacy laws is an excellent way to ensure that biometric data practices remain compliant. Legal counsel can provide insights into emerging trends and offer guidance on navigating complex regulatory environments.

For individuals, staying informed about biometric data laws will empower you to make informed choices about when and how to share your biometric information. Follow updates from trusted news sources, privacy advocacy organizations, and government websites to ensure you know your rights and the protections available.

Key Takeaways:

- **Limit biometric data use**: Only provide biometric data, such as fingerprints or facial recognition, when necessary.

- **Use devices with local biometric storage**: Choose devices that store biometric data locally rather than on a cloud-based server.

- **Stay informed about biometric laws**: Understand how laws in your country regulate the use and storage of biometric data.

- **Be cautious with third-party biometric services**: Only use biometric verification services from trusted sources and understand how they store your data.

- **Use multi-factor authentication with biometrics**: Pair biometric authentication with other forms of security, such as passwords or tokens.

BUILDING A PRIVACY-FIRST LIFESTYLE

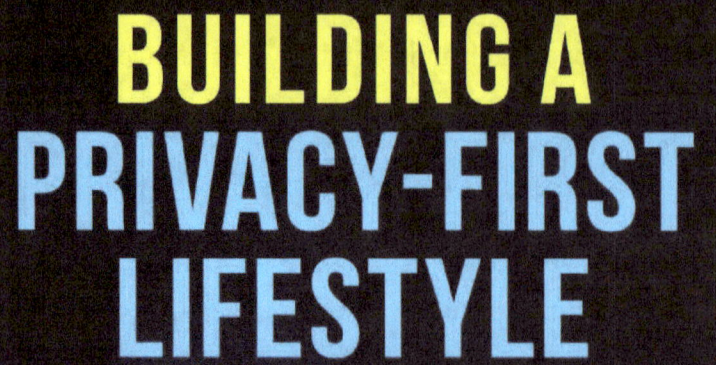

CHAPTER 8: BUILDING A PRIVACY-FIRST LIFESTYLE

In today's interconnected world, privacy isn't just about keeping your secrets safe—it's about preserving your identity, your data, and your peace of mind. Building a privacy-first lifestyle means incorporating practices that safeguard your information in both the digital and physical worlds. By developing habits that prioritize privacy, you not only protect yourself but also gain a sense of peace of mind, knowing that you are taking control of your digital footprint and contributing to a more secure and privacy-conscious society.

This chapter will help you integrate privacy into daily life through simple, actionable steps. Whether you're a seasoned tech enthusiast or someone just beginning to take privacy seriously, these strategies will provide a solid foundation for protecting your data. By following these strategies, you can feel more secure in your digital interactions, knowing that you are taking proactive steps to protect your privacy.

Overview: Integrating Privacy into Your Daily Routine

In today's digital era, where technology touches almost every aspect of our lives, privacy is no longer a luxury—it's a necessity. Whether sharing personal moments on social media, shopping online, or simply browsing the internet, our data is constantly being collected, stored, and analyzed. As a result, integrating privacy into your daily routine is crucial for protecting your personal information and maintaining control over how it is used.

Building a privacy-first lifestyle doesn't mean cutting yourself off from the digital world. Instead, it's about making conscious decisions in how you interact with technology. Privacy is a mindset, and once you start viewing your digital life through a privacy-focused lens, the actions you take to protect yourself will become second nature. From the apps you download to the information you share, incorporating privacy into your routine is about developing habits that keep your data safe without sacrificing convenience or enjoyment.

The Importance of Mindfulness in Privacy

Practicing mindfulness is one of the most significant aspects of integrating privacy into your daily life. Mindfulness, in this context, means being aware of your digital actions and understanding their consequences. Every time you log in to a new app, post on social media, or even browse the web, you create data. That data, in turn, can be used by third parties—advertisers, corporations, or even malicious actors.

By being mindful of these interactions, you can make more intelligent, more privacy-conscious decisions. For example, before downloading a new app, consider what permissions it's asking for. Does the app need access to your camera or microphone? Is it necessary for it to constantly track your location? Many apps request permissions that go beyond their core functions, and by denying unnecessary access, you immediately reduce your exposure to privacy risks.

Small Changes, Big Impact

Integrating privacy into your routine doesn't require a radical lifestyle change. Minor, incremental adjustments can have a massive impact on your overall privacy. The goal is to build privacy-enhancing habits over time, ensuring your digital life remains secure without feeling overwhelmed or complicated.

Start by addressing the basics, such as regularly updating your privacy settings on social media, email accounts, and devices. Then, move on to incorporating more advanced privacy practices, such as using encrypted messaging apps or browsing the web anonymously with privacy-focused browsers like Brave or Tor.

These small actions can lead to substantial benefits, as they limit the amount of personal information companies can track, reducing your digital footprint and keeping you in control.

Cultivating a Privacy-First Mentality

A privacy-first mentality involves shifting your perspective on how you use technology. It's easy to take privacy for granted, especially when services and platforms make sharing, storing, and communicating convenient. However, taking a privacy-conscious approach to these activities doesn't have to detract from the ease or enjoyment of using technology—it simply means being more selective and intentional about your interactions.

For instance, consider the amount of personal information you provide when creating new online accounts. Does the service need your phone number or birthdate? In many cases, you can leave out specific details, keeping your personal information out of unnecessary hands. You can also use aliases or separate email addresses for accounts that don't require critical personal data, further protecting your identity.

Another example of a privacy-first mindset is in your approach to passwords. Rather than reusing the same password across multiple platforms, create unique, complex passwords for each account. This minimizes the risk of various accounts being compromised in a breach, ensuring your data remains protected.

Protecting Privacy Beyond the Digital World

While much of the conversation about privacy revolves around the digital sphere, it's essential to remember that privacy extends into the physical world. Physical actions can influence digital privacy in a connected environment and vice versa. For example, be cautious about sharing personal information in public spaces where others might overhear sensitive conversations or see what's on your devices.

Additionally, maintaining privacy in your daily routine may involve more traditional actions, such as shredding sensitive documents before disposing of them or being mindful of who has access to your devices. If you're using shared or public computers, always log out of accounts when finished and avoid saving login information on browsers that aren't your own.

Similarly, consider the privacy implications of the smart devices you use in your home. Many devices, from smart speakers to home security cameras, are always listening or recording. Regularly check and adjust these devices' privacy settings and turn off features that collect unnecessary data when possible. By being mindful of both your physical and digital environments, you create a holistic, privacy-first lifestyle that covers all aspects of your day-to-day life.

Privacy as a Personal Responsibility

Integrating privacy into your daily routine involves taking personal responsibility for your data. In today's connected world, relying solely on companies or platforms to protect your information isn't enough. While many services offer basic privacy protections, the ultimate responsibility for your data lies with you.

This doesn't mean you need to become a privacy expert overnight. It simply means recognizing the role you play in safeguarding your information. Start with what you know:

- Regularly update your passwords.
- Be cautious with the data you share.
- Stay informed about privacy best practices.

As you gain knowledge and implement privacy-enhancing habits, you'll become more empowered to control your digital life.

Embracing Privacy as a Lifelong Practice

The digital landscape is constantly evolving, and so are the privacy challenges we face. This means privacy isn't a one-time effort—it's an ongoing practice. Just like how we maintain our physical health through exercise, nutrition, and regular checkups, we must retain our digital health by staying informed, updating our privacy practices, and adapting to new technologies.

Embracing privacy as a lifelong practice means continually assessing how you interact with technology and adjusting as needed. New threats emerge, new tools become available, and personal circumstances may change. By staying proactive and treating privacy as an integral part of your routine, you ensure that your information remains secure, no matter what new challenges arise.

Actionable Solutions: Updating Privacy Settings, Educating Others, and Staying Informed on Privacy Tools

1. Updating Privacy Settings Regularly

In the digital age, updating privacy settings on your devices, apps, and online platforms is one of the most essential steps to maintaining control over your personal information. Most apps, social media platforms, and web services have privacy settings that allow you to control what data is collected, how it is used, and with whom it is shared.

Why Regular Updates Matter

Technology companies frequently update their software and settings, changing how they collect and use data. Privacy policies and settings are frequently modified, often without users' awareness. As these platforms evolve, the default settings might expose more personal information than you'd like. For instance, a social media platform might change its default privacy settings to share your data with advertisers or allow your posts to be publicly visible rather than just your friends. You could share more than you intend if you don't regularly review and update your settings.

How to Update Privacy Settings Efficiently

- **Social media**: Social platforms such as Facebook, Instagram, LinkedIn, and Twitter collect vast amounts of personal data. Go into your account settings and adjust your privacy controls. Ensure your posts, photos, and updates are visible only to the chosen people. Also, look for options to restrict third-party app access, as many apps can gather data from your social media account without explicit permission.

- **Email and Messaging Services**: Many people don't realize how much data email providers and messaging apps collect. Services like Gmail, for example, analyze the content of your emails to serve targeted ads. Look for options to limit data collection and advertising personalization in your account settings. For messaging apps, review permissions, especially for apps like WhatsApp or Telegram, and turn off features that share your contact list or location.

- **Mobile Devices**: Mobile operating systems like iOS and Android allow apps to request access to features like your camera, location, contacts, and microphone. Review these permissions regularly and restrict any unnecessary access. For example, does a weather app need access to your contacts or microphone? Reducing these permissions protects your privacy and reduces your risk of being tracked without your knowledge.

- **Browsers**: Most web browsers have privacy settings that allow you to block cookies, prevent tracking, and stop websites from collecting your data. For additional protection, use privacy-focused browsers like **Brave** or **Firefox**, and consider installing extensions like **uBlock Origin** or **Privacy Badger** to block unwanted trackers and ads.

2. Educating Others About Privacy

Privacy isn't just about protecting yourself—it's about fostering a culture of awareness and responsibility. By educating others, especially friends, family members, and colleagues, you contribute to a more privacy-conscious society. There's a ripple effect: when more people adopt privacy practices, the ecosystem becomes safer.

Why Educating Others is Crucial

Many people are unaware of how much data they share online or don't know the steps they can take to protect themselves. Educating others empowers them to take control of their privacy and reduces the chances of their data being exposed. Moreover, when the people around you practice good privacy habits, it indirectly enhances your privacy. For example, if your friend has a habit of posting too much personal information about you online, their actions could also compromise your privacy.

Ways to Educate Others

- **Start Conversations**: One of the easiest ways to educate others is by starting casual conversations about privacy. You don't need to overwhelm people with technical jargon; instead, share simple tips like enabling two-factor authentication or avoiding public Wi-Fi for sensitive transactions. You could also discuss recent privacy breaches in the news and what steps people can take to avoid becoming victims.

- **Help**: Many people, particularly older generations, may not be comfortable navigating privacy settings or using privacy tools.

Offer to help them set up a password manager, review their social media settings, or install a VPN. This hands-on assistance can make a big difference.

- **Organize Workshops**: If you're passionate about privacy, consider organizing small workshops for your community, workplace, or online. You don't have to be a privacy expert to host these events; you can use resources available from organizations like the **Electronic Frontier Foundation (EFF)** or **Privacy International** to structure your presentation.

- **Discuss Privacy with Children**: With children spending increasing amounts of time online, starting conversations about privacy at an early age is essential. Help them understand the importance of protecting their personal information and teach them how to spot suspicious activity, such as phishing scams or inappropriate requests for personal data. As they age, ensure that these lessons evolve to keep pace with new challenges.

3. **Staying Informed on the Latest Privacy Tools**

The world of privacy is constantly evolving. New threats emerge as technology advances, and with them, new tools and techniques for protecting your data. Staying informed is essential to maintaining your privacy. Regularly updating your knowledge of the latest privacy-enhancing tools allows you to adapt your strategies and keep your data safe in an ever-changing digital landscape.

The Role of Privacy Tools

Privacy tools—such as encrypted messaging apps, VPNs, password managers, and anti-tracking extensions—are essential for building a robust defense against data breaches, surveillance, and hacking. These tools are designed to help you control who can access your data, and many are user-friendly enough for people without technical expertise to use effectively.

How to Stay Informed About New Privacy Tools

- **Subscribe to Privacy Newsletters**: Privacy-focused organizations and publications offer newsletters that provide regular updates on the latest tools, trends, and threats. Some excellent resources include the **EFF**, **ProtonMail's Blog**, and **Privacy Tools.io**. Subscribing to these newsletters makes it easy to stay informed without spending hours researching independently.

- **Follow Privacy Blogs**: Privacy experts often maintain blogs sharing their insights and recommendations. Blogs like **Schneier on Security**, written by security expert Bruce Schneier, offer valuable advice and reviews of privacy tools and technologies.

- **Use Open-Source Tools**: Open-source privacy tools allow the community to audit their code for security vulnerabilities whenever possible. Tools like **Signal** (an encrypted messaging app) and **VeraCrypt** (an encryption tool) are widely trusted because their source code is publicly available for review. This transparency makes them more reliable than proprietary tools whose internal workings are hidden.

- **Test New Tools**: Privacy tools are constantly evolving, with new apps and extensions released regularly. Don't be afraid to test new tools to see if they meet your privacy needs. For instance, if you've been using a VPN provider but heard about a new one with better security features, try it. Being flexible and open to new tools will keep your privacy defenses strong.

Actionable Steps:

- **Regularly review privacy settings**: Check privacy settings on all your devices and online accounts to ensure they are correctly configured.

- **Educate family and friends**: Share privacy best practices with those around you to help protect their data.

- **Use secure communication tools**: Always choose encrypted communication methods for sensitive discussions.

- **Stay up to date on privacy trends**: Follow news on the latest privacy tools, apps, and legal developments to keep your strategies current.

- **Adopt a privacy-conscious mindset**: Incorporate privacy awareness into your daily habits, such as using VPNs, encrypting files, and minimizing unnecessary data sharing.

CHAPTER 9: FUTURE TRENDS IN PRIVACY – WHAT'S NEXT?

Overview: Predict Future Developments in Privacy and Prepare for an Evolving Landscape

The rapid expansion of digital technologies has ushered in an era where data has become one of the most valuable resources in the world. As our lives are increasingly digitized, privacy concerns have moved to the forefront of societal, political, and technological discussions. The way personal data is collected, processed, and shared has profound implications for individual privacy. With innovations in artificial intelligence (AI), the Internet of Things (IoT), biometric systems, and blockchain technology, we are entering a period where privacy is more vulnerable and critical than ever.

As these advancements continue to accelerate, the very definition of privacy is being challenged and reshaped. Once defined primarily as control over one's personal information, privacy today involves safeguarding data from being exploited by corporate entities, governments, hackers, and even sophisticated algorithms. To navigate this evolving landscape, individuals and organizations must stay informed about emerging trends, adopt proactive strategies, and prepare for a future where data privacy is not just a legal right but an essential aspect of digital life.

Key Drivers of Change in Privacy

Several vital forces are shaping the future of privacy. First, technological innovation is the biggest enabler and the most significant threat to personal data protection. While emerging tools offer more robust privacy safeguards, they also provide new avenues for data exploitation. As AI becomes more integrated into everyday technologies, predictive analytics, facial recognition, and other forms of data processing will raise concerns about how deeply personal information can be mined and used without consent.

Second, regulatory frameworks worldwide are catching up with these technological changes. The General Data Protection Regulation (GDPR) in the European Union, for example, marked a turning point in how governments view corporations' responsibility in protecting consumer data. In the future, more countries are expected to implement similar laws, forcing businesses to comply with increasingly stringent privacy standards. However, balancing innovation with regulation will be delicate, as excessive regulatory pressure could stifle technological advancements.

Third, the global shift towards remote work, driven by the COVID-19 pandemic, has introduced new challenges in securing privacy. With millions of workers connecting from home, data privacy risks have multiplied. The security of virtual networks, cloud-based systems, and personal devices used for work has become a critical concern for employers and employees. As remote work becomes more permanent, companies must adopt more robust privacy policies and technologies to safeguard sensitive data from cyberattacks.

Privacy as a Fundamental Human Right

As we move into the future, privacy will increasingly be viewed as a regulatory obligation and a fundamental human right. Historically, privacy has often been seen as a personal issue—something to be managed by individuals themselves. However, as data breaches, corporate surveillance, and AI-powered data mining become more pervasive, there is a growing recognition that privacy must be protected at an institutional level. Governments, businesses, and international organizations must collaborate to establish global privacy standards that protect individuals' rights while enabling the free flow of information essential to innovation and growth.

This shift will be fueled in part by growing public awareness. Consumers are becoming more educated about how their data is collected and used, demanding greater transparency and control. Companies that prioritize privacy, offer customers clear, easy-to-understand policies, and can manage their data will gain a competitive edge. In contrast, businesses that fail to protect privacy face reputational damage, loss of trust, and potential legal consequences.

Technological Innovation and Privacy Tools

Technology will continue to play a dual role in shaping the future of privacy. On the one hand, emerging technologies like blockchain, encryption, and zero-knowledge proof systems will give individuals more control over their data. These tools will enable decentralized systems where users own their data, choose what to share, and interact anonymously if desired.

On the other hand, the rise of big data analytics, AI, and the IoT will make privacy even more challenging to manage. These technologies are designed to collect vast amounts of information, and without proper safeguards, they can easily be misused to infringe on privacy. For instance, AI systems used by companies for targeted advertising can analyze personal data to such an extent that they predict intimate details of individuals' lives, including their preferences, relationships, and even future actions.

Individuals will have to balance the benefits of new technologies with the risks they pose to privacy. For example, AI-driven tools offer convenience and personalization but also introduce significant privacy vulnerabilities. Companies using AI for data analytics will need to be transparent about their data collection practices and ensure they are protecting consumer privacy by implementing strong encryption and anonymization techniques.

Preparing for the Future: A Holistic Approach to Privacy

Individuals and organizations must adopt a holistic approach considering technological advancements and regulatory changes to prepare for the evolving privacy landscape. This involves a combination of education, advocacy, and privacy-enhancing technologies (PETs) that provide greater control over personal information.

1. **Continuous Education**: Staying informed about privacy risks and solutions will be essential in the future. Consumers and businesses must regularly update their knowledge of emerging technologies and privacy laws. Privacy is not a static issue; new risks emerge as technology evolves. By staying educated,

individuals can make informed decisions about protecting their data, while organizations can ensure they comply with the latest regulations.

2. **Advocacy for Stronger Regulations**: While technology can provide solutions, regulatory oversight will remain critical to ensuring privacy in the digital age. Strong privacy laws that protect consumers from data exploitation and provide clear guidelines for businesses will be essential. As governments continue developing these laws, individuals and organizations must advocate for policies that balance innovation and privacy protection.

3. **Embracing Privacy-Enhancing Technologies (PETs)**: As privacy concerns grow, there will be a surge in the development and adoption of PETs. These tools, such as encryption services, VPNs, and blockchain-based identity management systems, will allow individuals to protect their data more effectively. Companies, too, will need to integrate PETs into their systems to ensure that data is protected at all levels of operation.

4. **Building a Culture of Privacy**: Organizations must create a culture prioritizing privacy at every level. This involves training employees on privacy best practices, designing products and services with privacy in mind from the outset (privacy by design), and fostering an environment where transparency and accountability are emphasized. By building a solid privacy culture, businesses can ensure they are compliant with regulations and trusted by consumers.

5. **Global Collaboration**: Given the internet's borderless nature, privacy cannot be effectively managed on a national level alone. As more data flows across international borders, there will be a growing need for global cooperation on privacy issues. Governments, international organizations, and private companies must collaborate to create global privacy standards that protect individuals' data regardless of where they are located. This will be particularly important in addressing privacy concerns related to global digital services, such as social media platforms and cloud-based solutions.

Actionable Solutions: Staying Ahead of Trends and Embracing Privacy Innovations

As the digital landscape rapidly evolves, individuals, businesses, and governments must stay ahead of privacy trends to safeguard sensitive information. With technology's continuous advancement, responding to emerging threats and proactively adopting innovative privacy solutions is essential. The following strategies offer practical steps to stay ahead of the curve and embrace new privacy technologies that will become vital shortly.

1. **Proactive Adoption of Privacy-Enhancing Technologies (PETs)**

Privacy-enhancing technologies (PETs) are critical in the digital age for protecting personal data. PETs include tools such as encryption, anonymization, and secure multiparty computation, designed to minimize data exposure risk while ensuring the functionality of digital services. Simple tools like browser extensions or encrypted messaging apps offer immediate privacy benefits for individuals, but businesses and organizations can also leverage advanced PETs for complex data protection needs.

- **Key Examples**: Adopting end-to-end encryptions for all communications, using zero-knowledge proofs to verify transactions without sharing sensitive data, and leveraging differential privacy techniques to analyze large datasets without compromising individual privacy.

- **Staying Ahead**: Privacy-conscious individuals should monitor emerging PETs. Regularly updating digital tools and choosing services incorporating these advanced technologies will be essential to maintaining control over one's digital footprint. For businesses, investing in PETs will protect users and foster trust with customers.

2. **Fostering a Privacy-First Mindset**

In the coming years, a *privacy-first* mindset will be paramount to navigating the ever-changing digital landscape. This approach places privacy at the forefront of every online interaction, encouraging both individuals and businesses to critically assess the data they share, store, or process. Reacting after a breach occurs is no longer sufficient—preventive measures must be integrated into every facet of digital life.

- **For Individuals**: This means consistently opting for services that respect privacy. When signing up for new platforms, scrutinize privacy policies and ensure the service doesn't collect unnecessary data. Deleting unused accounts and minimizing the data shared online are vital steps.

- **For Businesses**, a privacy-first approach means building products with privacy in mind from the beginning—a practice often referred to as *Privacy by Design*. It involves embedding privacy into the system architecture at the development stage rather than as an afterthought. Businesses that design user-centric privacy controls will stand out as leaders in the digital age.

3. Continuous Privacy Education and Awareness

Technology evolves rapidly, and continuous education is the only way to keep pace with these changes. Privacy tools, policies, and threats will continue to change, making ongoing learning essential for staying ahead of trends.

- **For Individuals**: Staying informed about the latest developments in digital privacy will help them make well-informed decisions. Some ways to stay updated on innovations and trends are to join online communities, subscribe to privacy-centric newsletters, and follow leading voices in the privacy space.

- **For Businesses**: Regular staff training on privacy protocols and emerging threats is essential. Data security is often compromised due to human error, so ensuring that employees are up to date on best practices for data protection will reduce the risk of privacy breaches.

4. Embracing Decentralized Systems

One of the most promising trends in privacy innovation is the rise of decentralized systems. Unlike traditional centralized systems, where data is controlled by a single authority (like a company), decentralized systems allow users to retain full ownership of their data. Blockchain, for example, is one of the most prominent technologies driving this decentralization, offering transparency and immutability, two features crucial for ensuring privacy.

- **For Individuals**: Start exploring decentralized apps (dApps) that provide privacy-preserving alternatives to centralized platforms. For example, decentralized social media platforms enable users to control their data without third-party intervention.

- **For Businesses**: Companies should begin looking into decentralized data storage options, such as IPFS (InterPlanetary File System) or SIA, which offer encrypted and distributed data storage. These options reduce the risk of data breaches by making it harder for centralized attacks to target a single point of failure.

5. Advocating for Stronger Privacy Regulations

As new technologies emerge, privacy laws and regulations must evolve. Consumers and businesses can contribute to forming privacy legislation by advocating for stronger privacy protections and holding companies accountable for unethical data practices. Governments worldwide are slowly recognizing the need for stringent data protection laws, and citizens must be vigilant in pushing for these rights.

- **For Individuals**: Regularly exercising your privacy rights under existing laws (like GDPR or CCPA) is one way to remain actively involved. Keep an eye on emerging legislation and contribute your voice to public consultations on privacy issues whenever possible.

- **For Businesses**: Complying with privacy regulations is no longer just a legal obligation—it's a competitive advantage. Leading companies will adopt a proactive stance on compliance, not waiting for new rules to take effect but anticipating the direction of future laws and preparing accordingly. Companies can also take an active role by advocating privacy and shaping the global dialogue on digital rights.

6. **Implementing Zero Trust Architectures**

Zero trust is a security framework that assumes no user or system—inside or outside an organization's network—can be trusted by default. As privacy breaches become more sophisticated, this architecture has gained popularity for its ability to reduce vulnerabilities by constantly verifying and monitoring all systems and users.

- **For Individuals**: Using two-factor authentication (2FA) or multi-factor authentication (MFA) for personal accounts is a step toward embracing the zero-trust model in daily life. Additionally, avoiding using the same password across multiple platforms reduces the risk of compromise.

- **For Businesses**: Implementing zero trust requires a shift in how organizations approach data security. It involves real-time verification of users, monitoring for unusual activity, and limiting access based on necessity. This model is increasingly necessary as remote workforces and cloud services become more widespread.

7. Leveraging AI for Privacy Protection

Artificial Intelligence (AI) isn't just a threat to privacy; it can also be a powerful tool for enhancing it. AI can automate privacy tasks that are too complex for manual management, such as real-time data encryption, identifying unusual behavior that could indicate a breach, or automatically flagging suspicious activities.

- **For Individuals**: Consider using AI-powered privacy assistants to monitor your data across different platforms. Tools like Privacy Badger, which automatically blocks trackers, or apps that encrypt communications in real-time can help individuals maintain control over their data with minimal effort.

- **For Businesses**: Companies can benefit from AI by automating privacy management systems that handle large volumes of data. AI can track data access across departments, ensuring compliance with privacy regulations and identifying potential threats. Investing in AI-driven privacy tools will become a competitive necessity in the coming years.

8. Emphasizing Data Minimization

Data minimization is the practice of limiting the collection of personal information to only what is strictly necessary for a specific purpose. Collecting less data means there's less risk of exposing it in the event of a breach, and it's a growing trend in privacy-conscious organizations.

- **For Individuals**: Start by reviewing the apps and services you use and minimize the amount of personal data shared with each platform. Use pseudonyms or limit permissions for data access (e.g., location data) on your devices where possible.

- **For Businesses**, data minimization policies involve collecting only the essential data needed for operations and securely disposing of data when it is no longer necessary. This reduces the risk of breaches and builds trust with consumers, who are increasingly wary of companies that collect excessive data.

9. Enhancing Transparency with Consumers

Consumers demand greater transparency from companies about collecting, using, and protecting their data. Companies prioritizing transparency in their privacy policies and data handling practices will build customer trust and loyalty, which is increasingly seen as a competitive advantage in the digital age.

- **For Individuals**: Request access to your data from companies that store it and understand their privacy policies. Many companies now offer transparency reports or data management dashboards where users can review and adjust their privacy settings.

- **For Businesses**: Companies should create clear, easy-to-understand privacy policies and give consumers real-time access to their data through transparent reporting. Transparency should extend beyond legal compliance, offering users a more hands-on role in managing their privacy.

10. Preparing for Future Technological Disruptions

Privacy challenges will continue to evolve as future technologies such as quantum computing, augmented reality (AR), and 5G networks become more integrated into daily life. These technologies offer incredible opportunities but also introduce new ways to intercept or exploit data.

- **For Individuals**: Stay aware of emerging technologies and their privacy implications. For example, quantum computing could break traditional encryption, so it's important to follow developments in quantum-resistant encryption methods.

- **For Businesses**: Prepare for these technological disruptions by investing in future-proof privacy solutions. Quantum-safe encryption, secure 5G networks, and privacy-by-design principles for AR applications will ensure that companies are ready to face new privacy challenges as they emerge.

CONCLUSION: RECLAIMING YOUR DIGITAL LIFE

The digital world is vast, and navigating it safely requires vigilance and active participation in protecting your data. Throughout this book, we've uncovered the many privacy issues that modern technology brings into our lives, from corporate surveillance to government overreach. It's time to implement these lessons as we get everything together.

Taking Control of Your Digital Presence

The most crucial step in reclaiming your digital life is understanding that you have control. Companies and governments may collect data, but that doesn't mean you are powerless. Every click, post, and interaction online leaves a digital footprint, but some tools and strategies can help minimize exposure. By applying the practical solutions presented in this book, you can reduce the amount of personal information shared, take back ownership of your digital identity, and live with greater peace of mind.

Many people feel overwhelmed by the complexity of online privacy, often believing that securing their digital presence is a daunting task best left to professionals. But as we've discussed, reclaiming your digital life doesn't require advanced technical skills. It starts with essential awareness and a few simple steps.

The First Steps Towards Digital Privacy

Let's begin with what you've learned. From the very first chapter, the focus was on understanding the current digital privacy landscape. We talked about the threats posed by corporate surveillance, data breaches, and government overreach. These are big topics, but each one comes with practical solutions you can implement immediately.

Start by conducting a **personal data audit**. This might seem tedious, but it's one of the most effective ways to gain control over your privacy. A data audit means taking stock of what personal information is available online. Think about your social media accounts, the websites you visit frequently, and the apps you use daily. How much do they know about you? Consider searching your name in various search engines to see what information appears—this will give you an idea of the data available to others. Once you have a sense of what's out there, it's easier to make informed decisions about how to protect yourself.

The Power of Privacy Tools

Arming yourself with privacy tools is the next logical step. Many of these tools are user-friendly and designed for individuals with little technical background. For instance, a **Virtual Private Network (VPN)** can hide your IP address and encrypt your internet connection, preventing companies from tracking your online activities. This is especially important if you often connect to public Wi-Fi networks notorious for being vulnerable to hacking attempts.

Alongside VPNs, secure browsers like **Brave** or **Mozilla Firefox** with privacy extensions can block trackers and ads, giving you more control over who sees your data. You can also switch to search engines like **DuckDuckGo**, which don't track your search history or store your personal information. These are simple yet effective changes that can significantly reduce your digital footprint.

When it comes to communication, using encrypted messaging apps such as **Signal** or **Telegram** ensures that your conversations remain private and inaccessible to prying eyes. These apps offer end-to-end encryption, meaning only you and the recipient can read the messages, even if they're intercepted.

Password management is another cornerstone of digital privacy. We've seen how weak or reused passwords can lead to devastating breaches. A strong password manager like **LastPass** or **1Password can store** and generate complex passwords for all your accounts, adding another layer of protection without requiring you to memorize dozens of different login credentials.

Understanding the Risks of Oversharing

One of the most critical lessons from this book is understanding the risks of oversharing online. Social media has become an integral part of modern life, and while it provides many benefits—such as staying connected with friends and family—it also comes with privacy pitfalls. We've all seen how personal information can be harvested and sold to third-party advertisers, but fewer people are aware of how their posts can lead to privacy risks.

Consider the personal details you share online—birthdates, addresses, vacation photos, and even your location in real-time. All of these details can be exploited. Practicing digital minimalism is vital, which means sharing less and thinking critically about your post's long-term consequences. Adjust your social media settings to limit who can see your content, and be mindful about accepting friend requests or followers from people you don't know personally.

Controlling what you share makes it harder for cybercriminals to exploit your information. Simple things, like avoiding posts revealing personal identifiers or location tags, can significantly reduce the risk of misusing your data.

Staying Ahead of Cyber Threats

Technology evolves quickly, and so do cyber threats. This is why one of the core messages of this book is to stay informed and proactive. Hackers are constantly finding new ways to breach security systems, but by staying ahead of these trends, you can minimize your exposure to potential threats.

A key takeaway is that updating your software regularly is one of the simplest yet most effective defenses against cyber-attacks. Many people ignore prompts to update their devices or software, but these updates often contain patches for security vulnerabilities. Ensuring your system is always up-to-date reduces the risk of falling victim to an attack.

Additionally, recognizing **phishing attempts**—fraudulent emails or messages designed to steal your personal information—can prevent breaches. We've discussed the telltale signs of phishing, such as unexpected emails from unfamiliar sources, suspicious links, or requests for sensitive information. Identifying these red flags can keep you from accidentally compromising your data.

The Role of Corporate Responsibility

While individuals can take many steps to secure their privacy, corporations also play a significant role. Throughout the book, we've explored how companies profit from collecting, analyzing, and selling user data. This has led to widespread corporate surveillance, where your every click and action is tracked for profit.

However, corporations are not immune to public pressure. By choosing to support companies that respect user privacy, you can send a powerful message. Many companies now offer privacy-centric alternatives, such as **Apple's commitment to user data protection** or services like **ProtonMail, which** provides encrypted email without tracking your information. As consumers, we can influence corporate behavior by voting with our wallets. Supporting businesses prioritizing privacy is a meaningful way to advocate for broader change.

The Importance of Legal Rights and Advocacy

Another critical aspect of reclaiming your digital life is understanding your legal rights. In many regions, privacy laws are evolving to provide better consumer protection. For example, Europe's **General Data Protection Regulation (GDPR)** grants individuals greater control over their data, including the right to know what data companies hold on them and the right to delete that data.

But knowing your rights is just the beginning. Taking action to assert them is essential. For instance, you can request to see what data companies have collected on you or opt out of data-sharing agreements. Being proactive in exercising your rights ensures that companies are held accountable for how they handle your information.

Moreover, becoming involved in **digital activism** is an excellent way to contribute to the broader movement for privacy rights. Organizations like the **Electronic Frontier Foundation (EFF)** and **Privacy International** are dedicated to fighting for privacy and civil liberties in the digital age.

Supporting these organizations or participating in campaigns can amplify your voice and help shape future privacy policies.

Artificial Intelligence and Privacy

As we move deeper into the digital age, the role of artificial intelligence (AI) in privacy will only grow. AI can be both a tool for protecting privacy and a mechanism for violating it. For example, AI-driven algorithms help detect cyber threats and prevent data breaches. But on the flip side, these same technologies are used to track online behaviors and create detailed profiles for advertisers and governments alike.

The key takeaway is that AI will continue to influence privacy in complex ways, and understanding these dynamics is critical. As consumers, it's important to advocate for ethical AI practices—ensuring that companies use AI responsibly and respect user privacy.

Looking to the Future: Adapting to a Changing Privacy Landscape

Ongoing technological advancements will undoubtedly shape the future of digital privacy. Biometric data, artificial intelligence, and the Internet of Things (IoT) will create new privacy challenges that we've only begun to understand. However, staying informed and proactive will help you navigate these changes successfully.

As we look forward, one thing remains clear: digital privacy is an ongoing effort. There's no one-size-fits-all solution, and as technology evolves, so will the strategies needed to protect your personal information. The goal is to develop a **privacy-first lifestyle**—one in which privacy becomes a habit woven into your daily decisions and activities.

Final Call to Action: Protecting What Matters Most

At the heart of reclaiming your digital life is the recognition that privacy is about more than preventing annoying ads or data breaches—it's about protecting your autonomy, freedom, and personal safety in an increasingly connected world.

Now that you have the tools and knowledge, the next step is to put them into practice. Start small: update your privacy settings, audit your online accounts, and install privacy-enhancing tools. Then, build on these habits, ensuring that protecting your privacy becomes a regular part of your routine.

In a world where your data is the currency, safeguarding your privacy is one of the most important investments you can make for your future.

Key Takeaways:

- **Watch for developments in quantum computing**: Stay informed about the rise of quantum computing and how it may impact encryption and privacy.

- **Understand the role of blockchain in privacy**: Blockchain technology could revolutionize how data is stored and secured—explore its implications for privacy.

- **Prepare for AI's expanding role**: As AI becomes more integrated into daily life, be proactive in understanding how it affects privacy and data security.

- **Support privacy-forward technologies**: Look for technologies that prioritize user privacy, such as decentralized services and open-source software.

- **Anticipate future privacy regulations**: Governments around the world are beginning to strengthen privacy regulations—stay informed about new laws that could protect your data.

U.S. PRIVACY LAWS AND ACTS

1. **CCPA (California Consumer Privacy Act)**
   - A California state law grants consumers rights over their personal information, including the ability to request data deletion and opt-out of data sales.

2. **COPPA (Children's Online Privacy Protection Act)**
   - A federal law regulates the collection of personal information from children under 13. Requires parental consent for collecting and processing children's data.

3. **ECPA (Electronic Communications Privacy Act)**
   - A law that extends government restrictions on wiretaps to include electronic data transmissions, such as emails, phone calls, and electronically stored data.

4. **FERPA (Family Educational Rights and Privacy Act)**
   - A law protecting the privacy of student education records. It gives parents certain rights regarding their children's education records, which transfer to the student when they turn 18.

5. **FCRA (Fair Credit Reporting Act)**
   - A law that regulates the collection, dissemination, and use of consumer credit information, ensuring accuracy and privacy in credit reporting.

6. **FACTA (Fair and Accurate Credit Transactions Act)**
   - An amendment to the FCRA, providing additional protections against identity theft and regulating the use and reporting of consumer credit data.

7. **FOIA (Freedom of Information Act)**
   - A law that gives U.S. citizens the right to access information from federal agencies, with specific exemptions for privacy, security, and law enforcement.

8. **FISA (Foreign Intelligence Surveillance Act)**
   - A law that sets procedures for electronic surveillance and collection of foreign intelligence information, often raising privacy concerns in relation to national security.

9. **GLBA (Gramm-Leach-Bliley Act)**
   - A law that requires financial institutions to protect consumers' private financial information through privacy notices and security measures.

10. **HIPAA (Health Insurance Portability and Accountability Act)**
    - A law designed to protect the privacy of individual's health information and set standards for electronic health data transactions.

11. PPD-28 (Presidential Policy Directive 28)

- A directive aimed at balancing the privacy rights of individuals with national security needs, particularly in relation to signals intelligence activities.

12. Privacy Act of 1974

- A law that governs the collection, maintenance, and dissemination of personal information by federal agencies, giving individuals the right to access and correct their records.

13. RFPA (Right to Financial Privacy Act)

- A law that limits the government's ability to access an individual's financial records without their consent.

14. SCA (Stored Communications Act)

- A law that protects the privacy of communications stored by third-party service providers, such as email and cloud storage services.

15. Telemarketing Sales Rule (TSR)

- A law that regulates telemarketing practices, providing consumers with protection against fraud and privacy violations, including the National Do Not Call Registry.

16. USA PATRIOT Act

- A law passed after the 9/11 attacks that expanded government surveillance capabilities, including monitoring of communications and personal data for national security purposes.

17. VPPA (Video Privacy Protection Act)

- A law was enacted to prevent the wrongful disclosure of video rental records and other personally identifiable information related to video viewing.

18. Wiretap Act

- A law that prohibits the unauthorized interception of telephone, oral, and electronic communications, part of the broader ECPA.

U.S. PRIVACY-RELATED ACRONYMS AND DEFINITIONS

1. **API (Application Programming Interface)**
   - A set of functions that allows different software applications to communicate and interact with one another.

2. **BYOD (Bring Your Device)**
   - A policy that allows employees to use personal devices for work purposes, raising privacy concerns regarding company data on individual devices.

3. **CCTV (Closed-Circuit Television)**
   - A video surveillance system is often used for security purposes. It raises privacy concerns in public and private spaces.

4. **DLP (Data Loss Prevention)**
   - Tools and strategies used to ensure that sensitive information is not lost, misused, or accessed by unauthorized individuals.

5. **DNT (Do Not Track)**
   - A browser setting that allows users to opt out of tracking by websites and advertisers, though compliance by

websites is voluntary.

6. **DPO (Data Protection Officer)**

    - A role mandated by some privacy laws (such as the GDPR, although not required in the U.S.) to ensure compliance with data protection regulations.

7. **DPI (Deep Packet Inspection)**

    - A method of examining the data in network packets to determine content, raising privacy concerns due to its potential for monitoring user activity.

8. **EULA (End-User License Agreement)**

    - A legal agreement between a software provider and the user that outlines how the software can be used and any associated privacy concerns.

9. **IAM (Identity and Access Management)**

    - A system or framework used to manage digital identities and ensure that only authorized users can access specific systems and information.

10. **IoT (Internet of Things)**

    - A network of devices that collect and exchange data. Privacy concerns arise from the massive volume of personal information these devices generate.

11. **MFA (Multi-Factor Authentication)**

    - A security system that requires multiple verification

factors, such as a password and a fingerprint, to authenticate a user, adding a layer of privacy protection.

12. NDA (Non-Disclosure Agreement)

- A legal contract that prevents parties from sharing certain private or confidential information with unauthorized individuals or entities.

13. PCI-DSS (Payment Card Industry Data Security Standard)

- A set of security standards designed to protect credit card information during and after a financial transaction.

14. P2P (Peer-to-Peer)

- A decentralized communications model in which each participant acts as both a client and a server, sharing resources directly, which can lead to privacy risks in data sharing.

15. RFID (Radio Frequency Identification)

- A technology that uses electromagnetic fields to automatically identify and track tags attached to objects, raising privacy concerns about data collection.

16. SAR (Subject Access Request)

- A request made by an individual to an organization to access personal data held about them, a right granted under specific privacy laws like the GDPR (though not widely applicable in the U.S.).

17. TLS (Transport Layer Security)

- A protocol used to ensure privacy and data security between communicating applications over the internet.

18. VPN (Virtual Private Network)

- A service that encrypts internet connections and protects the user's browsing activities from being tracked by third parties, ensuring greater privacy.

19. XACML (eXtensible Access Control Markup Language)

- A standard for managing access control policies, often used in systems where data security and privacy are critical.

20. ZTA (Zero Trust Architecture)

- A security model that requires strict verification of every device or user attempting to access resources, whether inside or outside the network, to minimize privacy risks.

APPENDICES

Privacy Toolkit: A Curated List of Privacy-Enhancing Tools and Apps

As more of our lives are conducted online, protecting personal information from threats like data breaches, surveillance, and hacking attempts becomes essential. This toolkit provides carefully selected tools, apps, and resources that will help you take control of your privacy and enhance your digital security. The tools are organized by function, making finding what you need easy.

Privacy Toolkit: A Curated List of Tools, Apps, and Resources for Enhancing Digital Privacy

In this section, you'll find carefully selected tools, apps, and resources designed to help you protect your digital privacy. These tools are categorized by their primary function, making finding what you need easier.

1. **Secure Browsing**

Tools:

- **Brave Browser:** A privacy-focused web browser that defaults to block trackers, ads, and third-party cookies. It also supports Tor for anonymous browsing.

- **Mozilla Firefox:** A customizable browser with robust privacy features. Use privacy extensions like uBlock Origin, Privacy Badger, and HTTPS Everywhere to enhance security.

- **DuckDuckGo:** A search engine that doesn't track your searches or store your personal information. It's a great alternative to Google for privacy-conscious users.

2. **Virtual Private Networks (VPNs)**

Tools:

- **NordVPN:** This service offers strong encryption, a strict no-logs policy, and servers in multiple countries. It is ideal for securing your internet connection and masking your IP address.

- **ExpressVPN:** Known for its speed and reliability, ExpressVPN provides excellent security features, including DNS leak protection and a kill switch.

- **ProtonVPN:** A VPN service from the makers of ProtonMail, it offers a high level of security, with free and paid plans available. No logs are kept, and it includes strong encryption.

3. **Encrypted Messaging**

Apps:

- **Signal:** An open-source messaging app that offers end-to-end encryption for texts, voice calls, and video calls. It also includes self-destructing messages for added privacy.

- **Telegram:** Known for its privacy features, Telegram offers end-to-end encryption in its Secret Chats and self-destructing messages.

- **WhatsApp:** While widely used, WhatsApp offers end-to-end encryptions for all communications. However, it's essential to know its data-sharing practices with Facebook.

4. **Email Privacy**

Tools:

- **ProtonMail:** This secure email service, based in Switzerland, provides end-to-end encryption and does not log IP addresses. It offers strong privacy protection.

- **Tutanota:** This privacy-focused encrypted email service offers end-to-end encryption and a user-friendly interface. It's open-source and ad-free.

- **Mailfence:** This provider provides encrypted email services with features like digital signatures and encrypted calendars. It does not have third-party ads or tracking.

5. **Password Management**

Tools:

- **LastPass:** A password manager that securely stores your passwords in an encrypted vault, accessible with a master password. It also offers auto-fill for logins.

- **1Password:** Known for its ease of use and security, 1Password stores passwords, credit card information, and secure notes in an encrypted vault.

- **Bitwarden** is an open-source password manager that offers secure storage and password generation. It has both free and premium plans and strong encryption.

6. **Device Security Tools:**

- **Bitdefender:** A comprehensive security suite that offers real-time protection against malware, ransomware, and other threats. It includes privacy tools like a secure browser.

- **Malwarebytes:** This program focuses on detecting and removing malware, spyware, and other threats. It's a great complement to your existing antivirus software.

- **Sophos Home** offers advanced malware protection, web filtering, and AI-based threat detection in free and premium versions.

7. **Data Encryption Tools:**

- **VeraCrypt:** A free and open-source encryption tool that creates encrypted volumes and hides sensitive files on your devices.

- **Cryptomator:** A user-friendly encryption tool for cloud storage services. It encrypts your files before uploading them to services like Dropbox or Google Drive.

- **AxCrypt:** A simple yet powerful encryption tool that secures individual files and folders with AES-256 encryption. It's available for both personal and business use.

8. **Secure Cloud Storage**

Tools:

- **Tresorit is a highly secure cloud storage service with end-to-end encryption. It's designed for individuals and businesses and offers** file-sharing and collaboration features.
- **Sync.com:** This provider provides secure cloud storage with solid encryption and a focus on privacy. It's user-friendly and offers free and premium plans.
- **MEGA** offers end-to-end encrypted cloud storage with generous free storage options. All files are encrypted on the client side before they are uploaded.

9. **Anti-Tracking and Ad Blocking**

Tools:

- **uBlock Origin:** A lightweight, open-source ad blocker that blocks trackers and malware sites. It's highly customizable for advanced users.
- **Privacy Badger:** Developed by the Electronic Frontier Foundation (EFF), Privacy Badger automatically blocks trackers that violate your privacy.
- **Ghostery:** An anti-tracking tool that reveals and blocks trackers on websites. It also offers ad-blocking and analytics features.

10. Privacy Education and Advocacy

Resources:

- **Electronic Frontier Foundation (EFF):** A leading nonprofit organization defending civil liberties in the digital world. Offers guides and resources on privacy.

- **Privacy International:** This organization fights for the right to privacy worldwide and provides news, research, and tools to protect personal privacy.

- **The Tor** Project provides free software for enabling anonymous communication, including tools like the Tor Browser, which helps protect online privacy.

This toolkit provides a solid foundation for anyone looking to enhance their digital privacy. Each tool and resource is chosen for its effectiveness and ease of use, ensuring that you can take immediate steps to protect your privacy whether you're a beginner or an advanced user.

Glossary of Terms: Definitions of vital privacy-related terms

This glossary provides clear and concise definitions of key terms you'll encounter throughout the book. Understanding these terms is essential for navigating the complex landscape of digital privacy.

1. **Ad Blockers** are tools or browser extensions that prevent advertisements and tracking scripts from being loaded on websites, improving privacy and user experience.
2. **AI-Driven Surveillance**: The use of artificial intelligence technologies to monitor, analyze, and track individuals through the collection of large amounts of data.
3. **Artificial Intelligence (AI)**: The simulation of human intelligence by machines to perform tasks like learning, reasoning, and problem-solving.
4. **Automated Decision-Making**: AI systems make decisions without human intervention, raising privacy concerns in sensitive areas like law enforcement.
5. **Banking Alerts**: Notifications banks send to monitor suspicious activities on accounts, such as unauthorized transactions.
6. **Behavioral Biometrics**: A method of identification based on behavioral patterns, such as typing, walking, or interacting with devices.
7. **Big Data**: Huge datasets that can be analyzed to reveal patterns and associations, often used in surveillance.
8. **Biometric Authentication**: Using biometric data like fingerprints or facial features to verify an individual's identity.

9. **Biometric Data**: Personal data derived from physical or behavioral characteristics such as fingerprints or facial recognition.
10. **Biometric Data Breach**: Unauthorized access or theft of biometric data, which is difficult to change if compromised.
11. **Biometric Surveillance**: AI technologies monitor individuals based on physical characteristics such as facial or fingerprint recognition.
12. **Blockchain**: A decentralized ledger technology used for cryptocurrency and secure, anonymous transactions, enhancing privacy.
13. **Browser Extensions**: Small software modules added to browsers to enhance functionality, such as blocking ads or trackers.
14. **Chilling Effect**: When individuals alter their behavior due to fear of being surveilled, often limiting free speech.
15. **Consent for Biometrics**: It is a legal and ethical requirement that individuals give explicit permission before biometric data is collected or used.
16. **Cookie**: Small pieces of data stored on a user's device by websites to track behavior and preferences.
17. **COPPA (Children's Online Privacy Protection Act)**: COPPA is a U.S. law designed to protect the privacy of children under 13 by requiring parental consent for the collection of personal information. A real-world application of COPPA is seen on online platforms like YouTube and TikTok, where parents must obtain approval before collecting data from younger users. Companies that fail to comply face significant fines, as seen in the 2019

settlement where Google agreed to pay $170 million for violating COPPA.

18. **Corporate Surveillance** is the monitoring and collection of personal data by companies for purposes like marketing or user profiling.
19. **Credit Monitoring**: A service that tracks credit activity and alerts individuals of potential fraudulent actions.
20. **Cryptography**: Securing data by converting it into a code that can only be deciphered with the correct key.
21. **Data Anonymization**: Data anonymization is a process used to remove personally identifiable information (PII) from datasets, ensuring that individuals cannot be identified from the data. This is commonly used in industries like healthcare and marketing to allow analysis of trends without compromising personal privacy. For instance, a hospital might anonymize patient data before sharing it with researchers to study disease patterns, ensuring the individuals' identities remain protected.
22. **Data Breach**: An incident where unauthorized individuals access private or sensitive data.
23. **Data Encryption**: Converting information into a code to prevent unauthorized access.
24. **Data Minimization**: Collecting and storing only the minimum amount of data necessary to reduce the risk of misuse.
25. **Data Monetization**: Converting personal data into revenue, often by selling it to third parties for targeted advertising.
26. **Data Ownership**: The concept that individuals should control their data and decide who can access it.

27. **Data Protection Tools**: Software safeguards personal information from unauthorized access or breaches.
28. **Data Sovereignty**: The concept that data is subject to the laws of the country in which it is collected.
29. **Data-Driven Advertising**: Advertising tailored to an individual based on collected data, including browsing and purchasing behavior.
30. **Deep Learning**: A type of machine learning that uses neural networks to analyze complex data, often used in AI surveillance.
31. **Decentralized Identity**: A privacy-enhancing technology that allows individuals to control their data across platforms.
32. **Device Fingerprinting** is a method of identifying a device based on its unique characteristics. It is used to track users without cookies.
33. **Digital Footprint**: The trail of data users leave as they interact online, including browsing history and search queries.
34. **Digital Privacy**: The right of individuals to keep their online activities and personal data private from corporations, hackers, and governments.
35. **Encryption**: Encryption is the process of converting data into a code to prevent unauthorized access. In modern privacy practices, encryption is essential for securing sensitive information, such as personal data, credit card information, or healthcare records. For example, when you send an email, encryption ensures that only the intended recipient can read the message, as the data is converted into an unreadable format during transmission. This is

critical for maintaining confidentiality and preventing data breaches.

36. **End-to-end encryption (E2EE)** is a communication method in which only the sender and receiver can read the messages being transmitted.
37. **Ethical AI**: The practice of developing AI systems in a way that respects privacy, fairness, and the rights of individuals.
38. **Facial Recognition**: A biometric technology that identifies individuals based on facial features.
39. **Federated Learning**: A machine learning technique that trains algorithms across decentralized devices, improving privacy.
40. **FCRA (Fair Credit Reporting Act)**: The FCRA regulates how consumer credit information is collected, shared, and used. It ensures that credit reporting agencies provide accurate information and protect consumer privacy. A real-world application of the FCRA can be found in disputing errors on credit reports. If a consumer notices incorrect information on their credit report, the FCRA gives them the right to request an investigation and have the error corrected. Companies that fail to correct mistakes or protect credit data can face legal penalties.
41. **Fingerprint Scanning**: Identifying individuals through unique fingerprint patterns, often used for authentication in security systems.
42. **Firewall**: A security device that monitors incoming and outgoing traffic, creating a barrier between trusted and untrusted networks.
43. **Freedom of Information Act (FOIA)**: A U.S. law that allows citizens to request access to federal government records.

44. **General Data Protection Regulation (GDPR)**: A European Union law regulating how companies and governments handle personal data.
45. **Government Overreach**: Excessive use of governmental power, particularly in surveillance and data collection.
46. **Homomorphic Encryption**: An advanced encryption method that allows data to be processed without decrypting.
47. **Identity Theft Protection Services**: These services monitor personal information and assist in recovery if identity theft occurs.
48. **Incognito Mode**: This is a private browsing feature that prevents the storage of browsing history, though it does not fully protect against tracking.
49. **Internet of Things (IoT)**: A network of physical devices that collect and exchange data, such as smart appliances.
50. **Internet Protocol (IP) Address**: A unique number assigned to each device connected to a network, identifying and locating it online.
51. **Iris Recognition**: A biometric method that identifies individuals based on the unique patterns in their irises.
52. **Machine Learning**: A subset of AI that enables systems to learn from data and make predictions without explicit programming.
53. **Malware**: Malicious software designed to damage or disrupt devices and networks.
54. **Mass Surveillance** is the large-scale monitoring of individuals, often conducted by governments under the guise of national security.
55. **Multi-Factor Authentication (MFA)**: A security system requiring multiple forms of identification to access an account.

56. **Password Manager**: A tool that securely stores and manages passwords, generating intense, unique passwords for different accounts.
57. **Personal Data Audit**: A review of the personal data shared or collected by various platforms and organizations.
58. **Phishing**: A cyber-attack using fraudulent emails to trick individuals into revealing personal information or clicking malicious links.
59. **Pixel Tags**: Tiny, invisible images embedded in websites and emails to track user behavior.
60. **PRISM Program**: A secret U.S. government program that collects internet communications from major tech companies.
61. **Privacy by Design**: A principle in technology development prioritizes privacy from the outset, ensuring systems are built with privacy as a default setting.
62. **Privacy Policy**: A document that explains how a company collects, uses, and manages users' data.
63. **Privacy Settings**: Controls in apps, devices, and platforms that allow users to manage how their data is collected and shared.
64. **Private Browsing Mode**: A web browser setting that prevents the storage of browsing history, cookies, and site data.
65. **Predictive Analytics**: Using data, algorithms, and AI to identify the likelihood of future outcomes based on historical data.
66. **Quantum Computing**: A field of computing that uses quantum mechanics to perform calculations much faster than traditional computers.
67. **Ransomware**: Malware that encrypts files and demands payment for the decryption key to restore access.

68. **Social Engineering** involves manipulating people into revealing confidential information, often to gain unauthorized access to systems or data.
69. **Social Security Number (SSN)**: A unique identifier assigned to U.S. citizens and residents for tracking income, benefits, and identity verification.
70. **Spyware**: Malicious software that secretly collects data from a device without the user's knowledge.
71. **Strong Password**: A password that is difficult to guess, typically consisting of letters, numbers, and symbols.
72. **Synthetic Data**: Artificially generated data that mimics real-world data but does not contain personally identifiable information.
73. **Targeted Advertising**: Ads tailored to an individual based on their online behavior and past browsing data.
74. **Third-Party Tracking**: The practice of tracking users across websites by entities other than the one the user is visiting.
75. **Two-Factor Authentication (2FA)**: A security process requiring two steps to verify identity, such as a password and a code sent to a mobile device.
76. **USA Patriot Act**: A U.S. law that expanded government surveillance capabilities following the 9/11 terrorist attacks.
77. **Virtual Private Network (VPN)**: A service that encrypts internet connections and hides online identity by masking IP addresses.
78. **Voice Recognition**: A technology that identifies individuals based on the unique characteristics of their voice.
79. **Zero-Knowledge Encryption**: Encryption is when the service provider has no access to encryption keys, ensuring privacy.

Further Reading: Books, Articles, and Studies for Deeper Exploration of Digital Privacy

For those who wish to explore the topics of digital privacy, cybersecurity, and data protection in greater depth, the following curated list of books, articles, and academic studies will provide valuable insights and further understanding.

Books

1. "The Age of Surveillance Capitalism" by Shoshana Zuboff

This seminal work explores the digital economy's dark side, where corporations harvest and monetize personal data. Zuboff delves into how surveillance capitalism affects privacy, autonomy, and democracy, making it a must-read for anyone concerned with digital privacy.

2. "Permanent Record" by Edward Snowden

In this autobiography, Edward Snowden, the whistleblower behind the NSA surveillance revelations, recounts his journey and ethical dilemmas. It offers a compelling narrative on privacy's importance and government overreach's dangers.

3. "Data and Goliath" by Bruce Schneier

This book examines how governments and corporations collect individual data, often with little oversight. Schneier, a renowned security technologist, provides practical advice on how to protect yourself from pervasive surveillance.

4. **"Privacy in Context: Technology, Policy, and the Integrity of Social Life" by Helen Nissenbaum**

Nissenbaum's book introduces the concept of "contextual integrity" to frame privacy in the digital age. It offers a thoughtful analysis of how privacy should be protected based on the context in which information is shared and used.

5. **"Weapons of Math Destruction" by Cathy O'Neil**

This book investigates how big data algorithms can reinforce discrimination and erode privacy. O'Neil explores the ethical implications of data-driven decision-making and its impact on society.

Articles

1. **"The Privacy Paradox"** by Alessandro Acquisti, Leslie K. John, and George Loewenstein (Published in *Scientific American*)

This article discusses the "privacy paradox," where individuals express concern about privacy but behave in ways that undermine their privacy. It provides insights into the psychological factors influencing privacy-related decisions.

2. **"Why Privacy Matters"** by Neil Richards (Published in *Boston College Law Review*)

Richards argues that privacy is a foundational right in democratic societies. The article offers a legal and philosophical perspective on why privacy should be protected.

3. **"Big Data, Big Responsibilities"** by Vasant Dhar (Published in *Communications of the ACM*)

This article explores the ethical responsibilities of organizations that collect and analyze big data. It emphasizes the need for transparency and accountability in data-driven decision-making.

4. **"Understanding GDPR: An Overview of Europe's New Data Protection Rules" by Trevor Hughes and Omer Tene** (Published in *The Privacy Advisor*)

This article comprehensively guides the General Data Protection Regulation (GDPR). It explains the law's fundamental principles and implications for businesses and individuals.

5. **"Privacy and Human Behavior in the Age of Information" by Alessandro Acquisti, Laura Brandimarte, and George Loewenstein** (Published in *Science*)

This study examines the complex relationship between privacy, behavior, and decision-making in the digital age. It highlights the challenges of maintaining privacy in an increasingly connected world.

Academic Studies

1. **"Privacy and Information Sharing" by Daniel J. Solove** (Published in *California Law Review*)

Solove's study, focusing on privacy law, explores the legal and ethical implications of information sharing in the digital age. It thoroughly analyzes the tensions between privacy and the free flow of information.

2. **"The Impact of Artificial Intelligence on Privacy and Data Protection" by Mireille Hildebrandt** (Published in *Computer Law & Security Review*)

This study delves into the intersection of AI and privacy, discussing how AI technologies challenge existing data protection frameworks and proposing solutions for mitigating risks.

3. **"The Economics of Privacy" by Alessandro Acquisti, Curtis Taylor, and Liad Wagman** (Published in *Journal of Economic Literature*)

This study, which provides an in-depth economic analysis of privacy, examines how privacy concerns affect consumer behavior and the market dynamics of data exchange.

4. **"Digital Footprints: Opportunities and Challenges for Privacy in the Digital Age" by Paul Ohm** (Published in *North Carolina Law Review*)

Ohm's study discusses the implications of digital footprints for privacy, exploring how data trails can be used for beneficial and harmful purposes.

5. **"Contextual Integrity as a Theory of Privacy" by Helen Nissenbaum** (Published in *Washington Law Review*)

6. This study expands on Nissenbaum's theory of contextual integrity, offering a detailed framework for understanding privacy violations and protections in various contexts.

This list is just a starting point for those interested in digging deeper into digital privacy issues. Each resource offers valuable perspectives and insights, whether you're a privacy advocate, a professional in the field, or someone looking to understand better how to protect your personal information in the digital age. As the digital landscape continues to evolve, the need for privacy awareness and proactive security measures has never been more urgent. Remember, safeguarding your data is not just about protecting your information—it's about preserving your autonomy in a connected world. Stay informed, stay secure, and take control of your digital presence.

www.ingramcontent.com/pod-product-compliance
Lightning Source LLC
Chambersburg PA
CBHW052257220526
45471CB00001B/378